Swamplands
of the Soul

Marie-Louise von Franz, Honorary Patron

**Studies in Jungian Psychology
by Jungian Analysts**

Daryl Sharp, General Editor

Swamplands of the Soul

New Life in Dismal Places

James Hollis

For Taryn and Tim, Jonah and Seah. And for Rachel Erin.

I wish to salute Daryl Sharp for his vision and energy in bringing this series to the public. I also thank both him and Victoria Cowan for their deft editorial hands and their belief in the worth of my writing.

Canadian Cataloguing in Publication Data

Hollis, James, 1940-
Swamplands of the soul: new life in dismal places

(Studies in Jungian psychology by Jungian analysts; 73)

Includes bibliographical references and index.

ISBN 0-919123-74-0

1. Suffering. 2. Emotions.
3. Jung, C.G. (Carl Gustav), 1875-1961.
I. Title. II. Series.

BF531.H65 1996   152.4   C96-930170-7

INNER CITY BOOKS
Box 1271, Station Q, Toronto, Canada M4T 2P4
Telephone (416) 927-0355
FAX 416-924-1814

Honorary Patron: Marie-Louise von Franz.
Publisher and General Editor: Daryl Sharp.
Senior Editor: Victoria Cowan.

INNER CITY BOOKS was founded in 1980 to promote the understanding and practical application of the work of C.G. Jung.

Cover by Vicki Cowan (© 1996).
Inside: "Images from the Four Orders of Mystery,"
monoprints by Vicki Cowan (© 1996).

Index by Daryl Sharp

Printed and bound in Canada by
University of Toronto Press Incorporated

Contents

See final pages for descriptions of other Inner City Books

Introduction
The Search for Meaning

It is not given to us to grasp the truth, which is identical with the divine, directly. We perceive it only in reflection, in example and symbol, in singular and related appearances. It meets us as a kind of life which is incomprehensible to us, and yet we cannot free ourselves from the desire to comprehend it.—Goethe.

There is a thought, a recurrent fantasy perhaps, that the purpose of life is to achieve happiness. After all, even the Constitution of the United States promises "life, liberty, and the pursuit of happiness." Who does not long to arrive some distant day at that sunlit meadow where, untroubled, we may rest easy, abide awhile and be happy?

But nature, or fate, or the gods, has another thought which keeps interrupting this fantasy. The split, the discrepancy between what we long for and what we suffer as limitation, has haunted the Western imagination. To Pascal we are but fragile reeds that may easily be destroyed by an indifferent universe, and yet we are thinking reeds who can conjure with that cosmos. Goethe's Faust speaks of the two souls that contend within his breast, one clinging to this spinning planet and the other longing for the heavens. Nietzsche reminds us of that day wherein we discover and grieve the fact that we are not God. William Hazlitt observes:

Man is the only animal that laughs and weeps; for he is the only animal that is struck with the difference between what things are, and what they ought to be.[1]

Joseph Knecht in Hesse's *The Glass Bead Game* laments:

Oh, if only it were possible to find understanding. . . . If only there were a dogma to believe in. Everything is contradictory, everything is tangential; there are no certainties anymore. . . . Isn't there any truth?[2]

The litany arising from the gap between hope and experience is end-

---

[1] *The Oxford Dictionary of Quotations,* p. 243.
[2] Hermann Hesse, *The Glass Bead Game,* p. 83.

less. Whether to suffer it stoically, react heroically or whine about one's condition seems an onerous yet unavoidable choice. But Jungian psychology, and the disciplined practice of personal growth it promotes, offers another perspective based on the assumption that *the goal of life is not happiness but meaning.*

We may well experience moments of happiness, but they are ephemeral and can neither be willed into being nor perpetuated by hope. Rather, Jungian psychology, as well as much of the rich religious and mythological tradition from which it draws many of its insights, avers that it is the swamplands of the soul, the savannas of suffering, that provide the context for the stimulation and the attainment of meaning. As far back as 2500 years ago Aeschylus observed that the gods have ordained a solemn decree, that through suffering we come to wisdom.

Without the suffering, which seems the epiphenomenal requisite for psychological and spiritual maturation, one would remain unconscious, infantile and dependent. Yet many of our addictions, ideological attachments and neuroses are flights from suffering. One in four North Americans identify with fundamentalist belief systems, seeking therein to unburden their journey with simplistic, black and white values, subordinating spiritual ambiguity to the certainty of a leader and the ready opportunity to project life's ambivalence onto their neighbors. Another twenty-five to fifty per cent give themselves to one addiction or another, momentarily anesthetizing the existential angst, only to have it implacably return on the morrow. The remainder have chosen to be neurotic, that is, to mount a set of phenomenological defenses against the wounding of life. Such defenses too entrap the soul in an ever-reflexive response to life which grounds one not in the present but in the past.

An old saying has it that religion is for those who are afraid of going to Hell; spirituality is for those who have been there. Unless we are able to look at the existential discrepancy between what we long for and what we experience, unless we consciously address the task of personal spirituality, we will remain forever in flight, or denial, or think of ourselves as victims, sour and mean-spirited to ourselves and others.

The thought, motive and practice of Jungian psychology is that there is no sunlit meadow, no restful bower of easy sleep; there are rather swamplands of the soul where nature, our nature, intends that we live a good part of the journey, and from whence many of the most meaningful moments of our lives will derive. It is in the swamplands where soul is fashioned and forged, where we encounter not only the *gravitas* of life, but its purpose, its dignity and its deepest meaning.

Surely the most profound irony to befall the healing arts is the erosion of the idea of soul in the practice of psychology. It was just one hundred years ago from this writing that Freud and Breuer published their *Studies in Hysteria.* Late nineteenth-century physicians were forced to address the sufferings of those patients who could not find comfort and psychic cathexis in their religious traditions on the one hand, or be healed by the medical model on the other. A science of the suffering of the soul did not exist for those who increasingly fell between the cracks of modernism.[3]

Psychology was the last of the so-called social sciences to evolve, as Jung noted, because its raison d'être was theretofore sustained by the great myths and myth-making institutions. *Psyche* is the Greek word for "soul," and etymologically had twin roots: one the butterfly whose mysterious, beautiful, but elusive permutations metaphorically dramatize our experience of soul; and the other, from the verb "to breathe," is an analog of that invisible wind which enters at birth and departs at death.

How ironic, then, that modern psychology so often addresses only the behaviors which can be observed and converted to statistical models, or cognitions which can be reprogrammed, or biochemical anomalies which may be medicated. While all of these treatment modalities are significant and helpful, they seldom address the most profound need of the modern, namely, to render one's journey meaningful. Any therapy which does not address the issues of soul must remain superficial in the end, no matter how much palliation of symptoms it initially provides.

Jung suggested that neurosis "must be understood, ultimately, as the suffering of a soul which has not discovered its meaning."[4] Note that he does not rule out suffering, only the meaninglessness of life against which neurosis is a defense. Similarly he considered neurosis to be

---

[3] See my *Tracking the Gods: The Place of Myth in Modern Life,* chap. 2, for a fuller discussion of the modernist dilemma.

[4] "Psychotherapists or the Clergy," *Psychology and Religion,* CW 11, par. 497.

"inauthentic suffering." Authentic suffering is a realistic response to the ragged edges of being. The purpose of therapy is not, then, to remove suffering but *to move through it* to an enlarged consciousness that can sustain the polarity of painful opposites. As Aldo Carotenuto observes:

> Psychotherapy is not the construction of models according to which human suffering is channeled and labeled; it is the examination of suffering, the discovery of the dense fabric of correspondence between external and interior events which constitutes every life.[5]

Jung considered that a neurosis is not only a defense against the wounding of life, but an unconscious effort to heal such wounds. Thus one may respect the intent of the neurosis if not its consequences. Symptoms, then, are expressions of a desire for healing. Rather than repress them, or eliminate them, one must understand the wound they represent. Then the wound and the motive to heal may contribute to the enlargement of consciousness. Carotenuto also notes that "to decide to deal with suffering through psychotherapy, rather than appealing to an omnipotent divinity, is to opt for consciousness."[6] Such consciousness broadens and enriches us, though it may be dearly paid for.

The central idea that animates Jungian psychology is the reality of the unconscious. While this idea may seem commonplace, it is not in fact at the heart of those psychologies which are not psychodynamic in character, nor is it a common assumption in the experience of daily life for most human beings. Few have tumbled to the profundity of that autonomous force operating within, quite outside one's ability to comprehend, will away or even predict. Thus the obsessions, addictions and projections of complexes that originate from within ourselves are transferred to the outer world, unconsciously burdening others even as we complain of their oppression.

The thought that there is in each of us a vast, wise, natural power ought to be grounding and comforting when in fact it is often disquieting. The message of childhood experience, the message of vulnerability, powerlessness in the face of the environment, and the legitimization of

---

[5] *The Difficult Art: A Critical Discourse on Psychotherapy,* p. vii.
[6] Ibid., p. 3.

one's dependence, is overlearned, deeply ingrained, while the counter idea of personal freedom, personal responsibility, is intimidating.

What psychodynamic therapy seeks to promote is a new attitude toward one's psyche. What is intimidating in its power is also healing in its motive. To align oneself with those forces within rather than reflexively adjusting always to the powers without, thereby furthering our self-alienation, is to feel grounded in some deep truth, the nature of our nature. In those moments of contact with the deep truth of the person, the encounter with what Jung calls the Self, one feels the connection and support necessary to assuage the universal fear of abandonment. As Carotenuto puts it,

> Maturity implies not so much avoiding being abandoned, but in abandoning ourselves with few illusions. . . . If we succeed in bearing the anxiety of solitude, new horizons will open to us and we will learn finally to exist independently of others.[7]

As obvious as this notion of independence is, and as desirable as we may profess it to be, most of life is a flight from the anxiety of being radically present to ourselves and naked before the universe. Culture, as we have contrived it, seems but a divertissement, whose purpose is the avoidance of solitude. Indeed, next to the fantasy of immortality, the hardest fantasy to relinquish is the thought that there is someone out there who is going to fix us, take care of us—spare us the intimidating journey to which we have been summoned. No wonder we run from such a journey, project it onto gurus, never quite at home with ourselves.

Avoiding the dismal states of the soul becomes itself a form of suffering, for one can never relax, never let go of the frantic desire to be happy and untroubled, can never rest easy. Rather, one is unavoidably pulled down and under, frequently, painfully. Is not the natural rhythm of nature flux and reflux, ebb and surge? Do we not experience seasons, monthly menses, daily biorhythms, and spend up to a third of our lives in that underworld we call sleep? Is not such rhythm the nature of nature, the *natura naturata, natura naturans,* nature natured and nature naturing? Is not the antiphonal message of Ecclesiastes a celebration of such rhythm?

The ego, our conscious sense of who we are, is an affectively charged

---

[7] Ibid., p. 112.

cluster of replicated experience. It is the central complex of consciousness whose boundaries are fluid, malleable and easily violated. We need ego to conduct the business of conscious life, to mobilize psychic energy and direct it toward goals, to maintain a degree of self-consistency and continuity so that we can move from day to day, context to context. But the central project of ego is security which, understandably, stands over against the surge of unconscious material from within, and encounters the massive onslaught of energies from without. Given this project, this ineluctable, obsessive desire for security, the ego becomes a nervous nelly running about the parlor of life, picking up the clutter, dusting everywhere, making it even more uncomfortable to visit.

From the ego's narrow view of the world, the task is security, dominance and the cessation of conflict. From the perspective of depth psychology, however, the proper role of ego is to stand in a dialogic relationship with the Self and the world. Ego is to remain open, as conscious as possible and willing to negotiate. Jung called this ego-Self dialogue the *Auseinandersetzung,* which is the dialectical exchange of separate but related realities. The idea of the Self, as a reality transcendent and superordinant to the ego, is a recognition not only of the limitations of the nervous ego but of its place in a larger context. Jung's concept of individuation, the idea that the purpose of life is to serve the mystery through becoming an individual, is a profound contribution to our time, a myth for the modern as it has been called.[8]

Individuation obliges an ongoing dialogue between ego and Self. Out of their exchange the splits of the sundered psyche may partially heal. A functional definition of Self, then, would be the archetype of order within us. That is to say, the Self is an activity of psyche whose function is to further the development of the individual. One might say that the Self *selves*, or that we experience it *selving* through our somatic, affective and imaginal experiences. One could also describe the Self as a "willing matrix," that is, it is both teleological and contextual, both purpose and container. Psyche or soul, then, is simply our word for the mysterious process through which we experience the movement toward meaning.

---

[8] See Edward F. Edinger, *The Creation of Consciousness: Jung's Myth for Modern Man.*

So far as we know, ours is the only species which feels driven to find meaning. Such a drive is often painful, but it is autonomous and we cannot help but seek it. As Goethe noted in the epigraph at the beginning of this chapter, we can never comprehend this mystery, or it would not be mystery, but we frequently experience its intimations in the concretization of relationships, in the metaphors of dream life and in sudden epiphanies of depth. Wheresoever we intimate the presence of depth, in cosmos, in nature, in others or in self, we are in the precincts of soul.

While ego would like to encapsulate such depth in dogmatic certainties and quantifiable predictions, motivated by a desire for security, the mystery of which we are a fragmentary part is not only far beyond our capacity to engineer but beyond even our power to comprehend. We may stand in relationship to soul only through the imaginal world of the psyche, whether conscious or not, comprehensible or not. While we may seek it through ego-driven venues, ranging from theology to music to romantic love, we are more frequently pulled down into the swamplands where we least want to sojourn. Such descents are proof of the ubiquity, autonomy and essential mystery of soul.

While the idea of soul may be too amorphous for many, we must retain it precisely in order to honor its ambiguity, its elusiveness. Our ancestors lived in an ensouled world, which we today call animism. (Think on them the next time you knock on wood or say "bless you" when someone sneezes.) All of us in regressed states project psyche onto nature and onto others. Whether soul is in fact there is unimportant. What matters is that in such venues one may experience the depth, the intimation of mystery, which constitutes soul. Such intimations are strangely familiar, for they are encounters with what we carry as well. Like resonates with like. Baudelaire could recall a time when humans and nature were not so split:

> Nature is a temple from whose living columns
> commingling voices emerge at times;
> Here man wanders through forests of symbols
> which seem to observe him with familiar eyes.[9]

---

[9] "Correspondences," in Angel Flores, trans. and ed., *An Anthology of French Poetry from de Nerval to Valéry,* p. 21.

I live about a mile from the Atlantic Ocean to which, lemming-like, great masses migrate every summer. It is not to escape the heat, for air conditioning is generally available and much easier than fighting traffic and sand-flies. Surely it is because something in us resonates with the immensity of the ocean. Its awe-inspiring, trackless depths resonate, for we have the same depths within. Similarly, I live a few miles from the casinos of Atlantic City, annually the location most visited by tourists in the Western world, more than Disneyworld and more than the Big Apple. Surely there, too, onto green felt tables and clanking, blinking machines, soul has been projected. Surely there, too, a moment's transcendence, a transitory empowerment, an ephemeral encounter with the Other is sought. What one seeks is already coursing within but we facilely project it onto surf and sand, or the fantasy of life on Easy Street, the Boulevard of Dreams.

Soul is always present, albeit unconscious and therefore sought outside. Lost is the great insight of the poet Hölderlin: "The god is near, but difficult to grasp; however, where danger is, there Deliverance gathers."[10] Is it any wonder, then, that psyche pulls us back and down and in, to bring us back to soul?

The goal of individuation is not narcissistic self-absorption, as some might believe, but rather the manifestation of the larger purposes of nature through the incarnation of the individual. Each person, however insignificant in geopolitical terms, is the carrier of some small part of the *telos* of nature, the origin of which is shrouded in mystery but whose goal is conceivably dependent upon the enlargement of consciousness. If that be true, and I believe it is, then the task of individuation is wholeness, not goodness, not purity, not happiness. And wholeness includes the descent which the psyche frequently imposes upon the unwilling ego.

For most of our lives the dialectic of individuation pivots less upon the ministrations of the regal ego on its throne of hubris than upon the peasant folk within who grumble, have indigestion, and most often do not give a fig for the royal will. How many indifferent monarchs have been overthrown by the neglected little people? And just so, our unpredictable

---

10 "Patmos," in Angel Flores, trans. and ed., *An Anthology of German Poetry from Hölderlin to Rilke*, p. 34.

course through daily life. Despite the primacy of soul, the ego, frightened and bewildered, ignores, represses, denies, flees the swamplands. Yet much of our lives is lived from such regions, and much of the prison of neurosis is a denial of this realm.

Jung declared that he did not seek the cause of a neurosis in the past but in the present: "I ask, what is the necessary task which the patient will not accomplish?"[11] Invariably, the task involves some new level of responsibility, some more honest encounter with the shadow, some deepening of the journey into places we'd rather not go. Yet all of those psychic states have a soulful purpose. Our task is to live through them, not repress them or hurtfully project them onto others. What is not faced within is still carried as a deep personal pathology. To experience some healing within ourselves, and to contribute healing to the world, we are summoned to wade through the muck from time to time. Where we do not go willingly, sooner or later we will be dragged.

I had a friend during my years of analytic training who used to say, repeatedly, of any unpleasant situation, be it conflict with another or a troubling dream, "But what does it mean?" I found this very annoying, but she was right. *What does this mean?* Seeking the answer, we enlarge our horizons and live with greater dignity.

Soul work is the prerequisite not only of healing but also of maturation. Again, Carotenuto expresses it well:

> The ultimate purpose of psychotherapy is not so much the archeological exploration of infantile sentiments as it is learning gradually and with much effort to accept our own limits and to carry the weight of suffering on our own shoulders for the rest of our lives. Psychological work, instead of providing liberation from the cause of serious discomfort, increases it, teaching the patient to become adult and, for the first time in his life, actively face the feeling of being alone with his pain and abandoned by the world.[12]

In the following pages I will explore some of these underworld regions we have all experienced and long to escape. I will not offer solutions to the dilemmas they constitute, for they are not problems to be

---

[11] "Psychoanalysis and Neurosis," *Freud and Psychoanalysis,* CW 4, par. 569.
[12] *The Difficult Art,* p. 54.

solved. Rather they are omnipresent experiences of the journey assigned to us by psyche.

In a 1945 letter to Olga Froebe-Kapteyn, Jung observed that the *opus*, the work of soul, consists of three parts, "insight, endurance and action."[13] Psychology, he noted, can assist only in the provision of insight. After that comes the moral courage to do what one must and the strength to bear the consequences. While I shall offer some specific case examples, the paradigms they embody are truly universal. Most of the cases are real, though disguised; a couple are fictive. But those latter are more nearly true than those that are really true . . .

What follows is as much a series of meditations as it is a set of psychological observations. My purpose is to induce reflection and a personal assent to visit those swamplands more consciously. In the end, we have little choice, for, willing or not, we will spend much of our life there. Wrestling with these lower powers is not unlike wrestling with angels. As the poet Warren Kliewer expressed it in "The Wrestling Angel Challenges Jacob,"

> Of course you'd willingly stop groping for God
> if ceasing were one of the alternatives. . . .
> So grab me, hasty man, and we will worship
> with the frantic hopeless beauty of a fight.[14]

---

[13] *Letters*, vol. 1, p. 375.
[14] In *Liturgies, Games, Farewells*, p. 50.

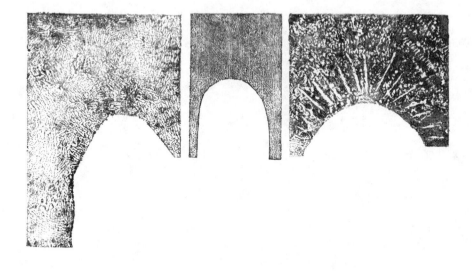

1
The Ubiquity of Guilt

When Ilse called for an appointment she specified two conditions. The first was that she have two consecutive hours, which would be the only time we met, and the second was that she mail me the Xerox of a photo to study in advance. I agreed. Three days later it arrived.

The photo was old and cracked but clear. It showed a woman holding the hands of two children. Apparently it was from some archive, for underneath a description was typed with the sort of uneven, occasionally faded or broken letters one remembers from the typewriters of one's childhood: "An unknown from Lublin leads her two children to the Majdanek Krematorium. (Possibly March, 1944)."

In the photo a woman, perhaps in her late twenties, dressed in a thin cotton coat, with wool stockings and black shoes, is facing to the left; her right arm is wrapped around a child of perhaps six, and her left arm is pulling a child of perhaps four from slightly behind her. I could not take my eyes from the photo of a photo. The woman's face was strained, alert, obviously anxious, but fixed forward. The child around whom she had her arm seemed enveloped in her embrace and was moving with her as if they were one. The younger child seemed terrified. Her eyes were wide, her body clearly holding back. Perhaps she was frightened by the noise, by the crowd, or what might be seen off to the left of the photo.

It was a moment in time, frozen forever. I felt the terrible irony of knowing what those in the photo could not yet know—that this was to be the last minutes of their lives, that they would be crowded into a shower, and that soon they all would be clawing each other and the absent heavens for untainted air. Could they know, could the woman know, what the children did not? The uprooting, the train-ride, the confusion, the father lost somewhere along the way, the terrible smell that hung in the air, and, once smelled, seared into the neurons, never to be forgotten by those who walked away—I was troubled by how much they knew. If only they did not know in the moment of this photo, if only this moment could still sustain hope, the thing with bright, fragile wings.

19

I woke early on the day of our appointment and knew I had been dreaming of that place where railroads converged, where Europe ended forever the frangible notion of moral progress. One detail of the photo haunted me. The smaller girl, the one lagging behind—the wool stocking on her left leg nearest the viewer was torn. She must have fallen and torn the stocking. I wondered if her knee had bled, did it still hurt her, and had her mother comforted her. Why I should worry about her knee while those awful doors yawned before her made little sense. Perhaps it was a form of moral metonomy. When one cannot take in the whole, one may focus on the small, the particular, the comprehensible.[15] I wanted to take that child and hold her, to touch that knee and lie to her and tell her it was like a bad dream and soon it would be all right. But I could not, could never reach her, and her fright perseverates down this ghastly century of protruding ribs, vacant eyes and nerves shot forever.

Ilse was in her late seventies. She spoke English perfectly, correctly, but I knew that her mother tongue was behind that slightest of accents. She wore a black skirt and white blouse and sweater, even though it was summer; one sensed it was her uniform of sorts, or that it was what she had always worn. She said, "I have asked for two hours today to tell you a story. You may stop me if you wish, ask questions, but I do not in the end ask anything of you, and this is the last time I will ever be here."

This is not the way therapy works, but I felt compelled to agree with her conditions for something seemed far more important at that moment than the rules of the game.

"Did you study that picture I sent you?" she asked.

"Yes, I have. I have even dreamed of it."

"So have I. That is what I want to talk about. I am the woman in that picture."

"But . . . I thought she was dead. The caption says they are walking into the Krematorium . . ." Even as I spoke I could see that the woman before me was the one in the photo. Fifty years is a very long time, but her face had the same eyes; she had not gained weight, her skin was still pulled tensely over the bones beneath her eyes.

---

[15] See below, p. 45, Rossetti's "The Woodspurge."

"I was the daughter of a physician in Lublin before the transports started. At first we paid no attention. My family was not Jewish. My father was too old to serve in the army any more and the war would not touch us. I was young and it was still far away. I wanted to meet someone and fall in love and get married and have a career too. When that photo was taken I was twenty-six, old not to be married then, and worried that I wouldn't find someone."

"But how did you get to Majdanek? You weren't Jewish. You were safe."

"I look back on it now as the most foolish of things. I had gone to the open market on a Friday morning to get vegetables for my mother. It was that day that the *Einsatzkommando* had their *Aktion*. They knew the Jews would be at the market before the Sabbath began. They surrounded the market place even as other units went to the Jewish quarter and closed off whole blocks at a time. I was caught up in it."

"Didn't you tell them . . .?"

"Of course, from the beginning, I said I am a Christian, *nicht Jude,* but others were saying that too. And they laughed and pushed all of us on to trucks."

As she spoke, she seemed back in that place. I cannot say that she was frightened, as such, but she was there in her mind's eye. Perhaps she was dissociated in some fashion, but she was really there. She told me how she had been driven with the others, protesting all the while, to the *Hauptbahnhof* and loaded on a railway car. A few hours later, terrified but stupefied, they arrived at a trestle outside of a place called *K-Z Lager Majdanek,* one of the extermination centers of the so-called *Endlösung*— the bankruptcy of centuries of civilizing culture in a mad projection of the intolerable in ourselves onto "those out there."

I knew not to speak. She continued and told me how they were pushed before an officer who motioned them right or left. Which line led to the ovens, and which to a pestilential life in the barracks with the typhus, the brutal work, the eight hundred calories a day, and finally the collapse of the spirit in a body already broken?

In front of Ilse a mother held her two children, one stunned into silence, one crying. When they came before the officer he smiled at her and pointed to the right, but the children to the left. The woman screamed and clung to her children, but she was pulled away and sent to join the smaller group off to the right. The two children stood there, afraid to move, puzzled by their mother's cry. Then Ilse stepped before the officer. At the critical moment, at the "Selection," she screamed out in my office, as she must have at that moment, "I am a Christian; *Ich bin nicht Jude!*" The officer replied that it was too late for a conversion and that many people said they were Christians. Ilse then recounted how she named her father, her father's father and the long line of physicians known in the area, after one of whom a Lublin hospital had been named.

The officer paused and then said, "*Ja, stimmt,* but you have seen too much here to ever go back. Take these two children to the door of the bathhouse and get them inside and then you join the others. But you will work with them, and you will never leave here."

"I cannot tell you how happy I was for that moment," said Ilse. "I would not have to go in there. I would work. I would live a while longer. I pushed the children. One hung on to me; the other I had to pull along. It was at that moment that someone took that picture you see. I do not remember anyone being there with a camera. I was so happy that I would live. I pulled the children along and took them to the entrance to the bathhouse. There *Capos* from the prisoners themselves pulled the children through the doors. That was the last I ever saw of them."

Again, at that moment, I could see she was there, relieved somehow for the respite that would be hers. She slumped back in her chair, silent for perhaps two minutes, and then continued. She told me of life in the camp, how despite having only a reprieve she had survived the brutal work, the shaved head, the daily gruel with the resilience of her youthful body to draw upon. When the Russians came to liberate the camp only a few hundred walking skeletons were left, and many of them died soon after from disease and the continued effects of starvation.

"I moved to Warsaw after the war. Many of my father's family lived in America, so I was able to get a visa to live in Detroit. For years I would not think of those days. I never married. I was afraid I would have a child. I knew I had lost the possibility to love. I worked in libraries all these years until the day, four years ago, I came across this photo in a history of the war. I can never tell you how it all came back, the noise, the smell, the fear . . . but most of all the thrill that I was going to live a bit longer."

Now I thought I knew why she was here. I had worked with survivors before, and worse than what today we call "post-traumatic stress disorder" was survivor guilt. Often the guilt was so great that they had decided, consciously or unconsciously, to die unto life. So they walked around emotionally anesthetized, living in silence and suspicion, never feeling the tang and savor of being alive.

But she said, "I do not want anything from you. I don't want you to say anything to me. I want you only to have listened. I became a Jew a few years ago, or tried, but it didn't take. I couldn't believe in their God who betrayed them. But I did hear of the tradition of the *melamed vovnikim,* the belief that no matter how bad things are on this earth, that God has left twenty-four just persons, and if you tell them your story you will be heard unto the heavens."

"I can't say I am one of the Just, Ilse."

"I will keep telling the story of this photograph in any case. Perhaps you are, perhaps not. I still have some time left and there are others I must find."

As she left I told her I could not accept money from her, for I felt that I had not been able to help. She asked, then, that I keep the photograph instead. I did, and have it still. She walked out of my office and I never saw her again, though there is not a day I do not think of her.

Viktor Frankl once observed that as terrible as Auschwitz was, it was only a hyperbole of everyday life.[16] Frankl has the right to make that observation; I do not. But I think I understand his point that every day large issues of soul were up for grabs, and the best, he said—those who shared their food and refused to brutalize their neighbors as they were brutalized—did not survive. So Ilse's photo is the story of us all, even those of us who have lived safe lives. None of us can say what we would have done in such a circumstance as fate placed her; we all have our own memories of moments of moral cowardice, and none of us can blame her

---

[16] *Man's Search for Meaning,* p. 92.

for her fierce desire to live. And yet all of us understand why she still wanders, a modern mariner, with the photo of her guilt around her neck, seeking the Just, seeking to have been heard, if not absolved.

Guilt sits like a large black bird on the shoulders of most of us. Jung's concept of the shadow reminds us all of our participation in the forbidden, our egotism, our narcissism and cowardice. And who does not remember the helpful words of the Latin poet Terrence, *"Ego sum humanum. Nihil a me humanum alienum."* I am human, and nothing human is alien to me. But that large black bird still sits there and caws cacophonously just when we wish to celebrate, to be free, unfettered by the past. It caws and erodes the moment, and all slips back and down into the past with its attendant shame.

It may be useful in our reflection to differentiate the concept of guilt further, for like so many concepts, many different sorts of experience may be subsumed under one blanket term. We need rather carefully to distinguish between:

1. Real guilt as a form of responsibility.
2. Guilt as the inauthentic defense against angst.
3. Existential Guilt.

Real Guilt As Responsibility

While the judicial systems of all nations recognize the possibility of diminished guilt, where one is under a certain age or mentally impaired, no reader of this book will quite fit those categories. If the task of individuation obliges the enlargement of consciousness, none of us can afford the casual comfort of innocence. No one who is conscious can claim innocence, either on the personal level, or, as Albert Camus made so clear in *The Fall,* on the collective level. Each of us is a part of the fabric of that same society which made the Holocaust, which perpetuates racism, sexism, ageism, homophobia, whether we actively collude or not.

Thus, part of the legitimate development of the individual is the appropriate acknowledgment of guilt, which is to say the acceptance of responsibility for the consequences of one's choice, however unconscious one was at the time.

The essence of Greek tragedy was the recognition that there are forces within the culture, or within the individual, which bring one to make choices through which others may suffer. In most tragedies the Chorus, representing not only the authorial perspective but also collective wisdom, witnesses the workings of fate in setting up possibilities and wounding the protagonist. As a result of what the Greeks called *hamartia*—often translated as "the tragic flaw," but I prefer "the wounded vision"—the individual makes choices whose consequences cannot be foreseen. Through suffering, the individual may then come to redemption by acknowledgment, penance and a reconstitution of right relationship to the gods.

In *The Middle Passage* I suggested that such a wounded vision was an inevitable concomitant of childhood experience and brought the individual, often at midlife, to a collision with the reality of many false choices. Two brief illustrations may help.

Richard Nixon was deeply wounded by the deprivations of his childhood. He responded to those deprivations by an over-compensated power drive for recognition and respect. Having attained what he sought, the wounded vision remained unconscious and he made choices which brought his public repudiation. The third act of Richard Nixon was never written. He never admitted to more than a few mistakes in judgment, and averred that such was the way politics works. He never saw that he was the source of his own bad choices and, humbling as that might be, he was denied the peace that comes from reestablishing right relationship to the moral fabric.

On the other hand, as the 1993 film *Quiz Show* depicts, Charles Van Doren was the scion of a famous American academic family. But he sought his famous father's approval in vain and could only come in second best while competing intellectually. The temptation of a rigged quiz show brought him the money, celebrity and acclamation his father could never have attained; it also brought about his public exposure and humiliation. To his credit, he appeared before the congressional investigative committee and accepted full responsibility for his choices and acknowledged where he had lost his moral compass.

We all may find something familiar in these two examples. To say that I have erred, that I am guilty of bad choices and their hurtful consequences, is not only the beginning of wisdom, but also the only path that can ultimately lead to release.

Those who grow up in a community of belief, knowing the sacrament of the confessional, have an opportunity for release from the past. For not only does the black bird of guilt erode the quality of the present, it ties us always to the past as well. Carrying the burden of the past is exhausting and degrades our power to make new choices.

But most moderns do not have the confessional as a possibility, either because they are of another tradition or because they can no longer draw upon the implicit faith such a transaction requires. Ilse will forever make her round in search of the Just for, finding one, she might not even then have the power of belief which makes acceptance of grace possible. Nonetheless, even those outside the sacramental history of the confessional may be instructed by what might be called "the three R's": recognition, recompense and release.

For one to begin to deal with guilt in a mature fashion, *recognition* is essential. Consciousness involves the recognition of harm done to self or other. It may be that at first one may not legitimately understand the harm done, but when such recognition is available, then consciousness must acknowledge that, yes, I did that, caused that, am responsible for that. The sociopath, and those with certain other character disorders, whose ego capacity is so damaged that they cannot take responsibility, may lie not only to others but to themselves as well, repeatedly projecting responsibility outside themselves.

It is a widespread misperception that much of psychotherapy is spent blaming parents, or socioeconomic conditions, rather than dealing with the present. While much of our character is in fact shaped by those formative experiences, the essence of therapy is the acknowledgment of responsibility for one's choices, for one's life. Anything else is an evasion of genuine adulthood. Such recognition may be humbling, even shattering, but further denial or unconsciousness adheres one to the past without hope of change. Thus much of the work of Twelve Step programs is based on ending the denial, accepting the responsibility for one's life, and, where possible, recompensing those injured.

Recompense is only possible on occasion. Many things done cannot be undone. Ilse could never bring back the children. She tried to adopt their faith, but such a sincere move was in the end ineffective, even irrelevant. She refrained from having children herself, perhaps because she could not bear to see the children of Majdanek in their faces, perhaps because she felt the need to punish herself. But direct recompense was not possible for her. When recompense is possible it is essential to recognize that it only makes sense in the context of genuine contrition. Anything less would be a materialization of soul and in the end not effective. In most cases the recompense one offers is symbolic, no less real for that, but clearly an act of psychological return for that which has been taken.

How and why our penal system is so ineffective may be partially clear here. Even the words *penitentiary* and *reformatory* are based on the idea that if a person were exiled from the psychological support of the collective, he or she would be "penitent" and moral "reformation" would occur. But the system we have is in fact punitive and rarely addresses the question of how a legitimately convicted person can be helped to become conscious of wrongdoing and assume responsibility for it, rather than blaming society or simple bad luck.

When contrition is genuine, when recompense actually or symbolically has transpired, then one may experience the grace of *release*. For those who may still draw upon the sacrament of the confessional, the priest is able to act as divine intermediary and effect the forgiveness, the release. This release is seen as an act of God which cannot be earned but is founded on contrition; this is called grace. For those not in such a religious community, finding grace is no easy thing. Still, the tripartite process of recognition, recompense and release may still be available to those who seek the enlargement of consciousness. Such enlargement obliges one to acknowledge one's shadow, but in owning it, taking responsibility for it, one begins to move into the world in new ways.

Jung has written eloquently of the healthy acknowledgment of guilt. It does not signify denial or avoidance, and it is certainly not remaining stuck in the past.

> Such a man knows that whatever is wrong in the world is in himself, and if he only learns to deal with his own shadow he has done something real for the world. He has succeeded in shouldering at least an infinitesimal part of

the gigantic, unsolved social problems of our day. . . . How can anyone see straight when he does not even see himself and the darkness he unconsciously carries with him into all his dealings.[17]

Guilt As a Defense Against Angst

Much of the time, perhaps usually, what we call guilt is not real guilt, as defined above. It is more often a queasy feeling, or a freezing of the extremities, or even a lightheadedness. Curiously enough, so often this particular experience is expressed somatically, which is always a clue that a complex has been hit. The signs of an activated complex (discussed in greater depth below, chapter eight) are that the amount of energy generated is in excess of the reasonable requirement of the situation, and that one experiences a somatic invasion, a feeling state in the body. These are clues that one is in fact experiencing a movement of psyche beneath the level of consciousness.

Moreover, much of what we call guilt is a defense against a greater angst; it is an epiphenomenal response to the experience of anxiety with which it is so closely identified as to be indistinguishable at that moment. For example, we hear people saying they feel guilty when they say no to someone, or when they are angry, or for not being the perfect parent. Such feelings have been slowly conditioned since childhood. The child's natural narcissism acts out all desires spontaneously, immediately running into the phalanx of the adult world with its unlimited power to punish or to withhold approval and affection. No child can last long in such a wasteland, and quickly learns to curb unacceptable impulses.

One man recalled singing on the porch of his home when he was around six years old. His mother screamed at him not to make such "noise" and he vowed he would never sing again. Later, in a required high school singing class, he was tongue-tied. When the instructor learned that he was literally unable to sing, the boy was allowed to stand silent in the back row of the chorus all semester and given a passing grade. As an adult, this man would not even risk singing in the shower. The issue may seem rather trivial, certainly when compared with more serious child abuse, but it is illustrative of the power of an internalized

---

[17] "Psychology and Religion," *Psychology and Religion,* CW 11, par. 140.

encounter with the omnipotent parent. From such encounters with the power principle, inevitable in the socialization of all of us, one begins to internalize restraints against one's impulses. In time one may even be defended against the primacy of any affectively charged motive, and, finally, come to lose contact with the reality of one's feelings.

What is called guilt, then, is often a child's protective, reactive feeling state. The queasy feeling, the sudden coldness, are reflexive memories of visitations to the wasteland of parental disapproval. It is as if, when a natural impulse arises, anger for example, a hand reaches out like a governor in a car and throttles the impulse. Such a reflexive reaction can so govern a person's life that he or she will suffer considerable self-alienation. Feeling guilty for saying no, for example, is really a defense against the possibility that the Other will be displeased, thereby activating the immense reservoir of emotion we all carry.

Such inauthentic guilt may be aligned against resentment of others, jealousy, rage, lust and the whole host of shadow material. Jung noted that a shadowless person, which is to say one unconscious of and highly defended against the shadow, is a shallow person. Most of us were conditioned to be nice rather than real, accommodating rather than authentic, adaptive rather than assertive. Imagine a Twelve Step program for "recovering nice persons," where one describes how he or she was reflexively nice during the past week and lived to regret it; or, when deciding not to be nice, how guilty one felt.

Guilt as a defense against a deeper angst reflects a lack of permission to be oneself. It reflects the incalculable power of early conditioning. And it offers a chance for persons to recover the initiative in their lives. In such moments of guilt one is invited to ask, "Against what am I defending myself?" Usually the matter will boil down to the fear that someone else might not be happy with one's decisions.

In the real world, to be a person of value rather than an emotional chameleon, choices perforce must be made and pleasing others cannot be at the top of the agenda. The angst that surges from below is experienced as overwhelming precisely because it dates from the time of one's great childhood vulnerability. Because that energy is never lost but resides in the unconscious, it can spring forth with paralyzing power. At that moment one is not in the present but in the disempowered state of the child. One forgets that since that time an adult has evolved who, when acting consciously, is perfectly capable of making decisions of value and who can live, if it proves necessary, with the displeasure of others.

Since such guilt is inauthentic, not the courageous acknowledgment of wrong done to others, it is essential to work through the epiphenomenal angst to achieve adulthood. Being blocked by guilt is still to be stuck in childhood. When we become conscious of the origin of that queasy feeling, such stuckness is no longer unconscious and no longer acceptable.

Existential Guilt

The last form of guilt is existential in character; it is an unavoidable concomitant of being human. For example, we understand that the principle which underlies life is death. Not only are life and death the systole and diastole of the cosmos, but all life depends on killing. We kill animals to survive. If we choose to be vegetarian, we slay plant life. If we stop eating we commit suicide. For this reason our ancestors offered "grace" at meals, that is, not only thanks but the acknowledgment of the principle that what we are about to eat has derived from an act of slaying. Ancient cultures, for the same reason, offered prayers before and after the hunt, and during consumption of the food, in order to acknowledge their participation in the death-rebirth cycle of the Great Mother archetype.[18]

Even if we ignore our participation in the cycle of sacrifice, we still all compete in the market place and take something for ourselves from others. If one part of the globe prospers it may be at the expense of another part. If the economic indices climb it may be at the expense of the environment, and so on. This dilemma is inherent in the human condition. It is intimated in many of the foundation myths of religious traditions. In the Judeo-Christian tradition, for example, the guilt of Adam and Eve is inevitable, unavoidable and systemic. They eat of the Tree of Knowledge. Once they are no longer infantile they are obliged to see their naked truths, that they live at the expense of the other, that they are divided in their sensibility, responsible for their choices no matter how much they protest their innocence. Their expulsion from Eden is really

---

[18] See my *Tracking the Gods,* pp. 59-65.

the necessary departure from naiveté, from infantile unconsciousness, from consequence-free choices. Thereafter they are obliged to suffer the fact that many of their choices will not be between good and bad, but between all sorts of moral grays. They will need to acknowledge their moral ambiguity and their personal and cultural duplicity.

Again, one thinks of Albert Camus' novel *The Fall*. Though Algerian born, as a French writer Camus was immersed in the Judeo-Christian tradition, and he could think of no more powerful metaphor for the modern who on the one hand has seen the Holocaust emerge from his civilization, and on the other has experienced his own moral slipperiness. Out of such necessary recognition one falls from the pinnacle of self-inflation, to be sure, but with it comes the beginning of consciousness, the necessary humbling in the descent to the moral swampland, the enlarged capacity for psychological richness.

Such a person, humbled, is not only more interesting but more fully human. This must have been what Blake saw when he read *Paradise Lost*. "Milton," he wrote, "was of the Devil's Party though he knew it not."[19] Satan was, in his moral complexity, far more interesting than the vanilla Deity. Satan was guilty of hubris, to be sure, but his psychology is in fact more like ours than not, his dilemma and existential guilt somehow richer for all its ruin.

Luigi Zoja, in his book *Growth and Guilt*, tracks the rhythm of *hubris* and *nemesis*, of the human capacity for arrogating the prerogatives of the gods to themselves, and suffering the cosmic reaction which brings about the humbling, the leveling, the restoration of the balance (called *sophrosyne* by the Greeks). History, Zoja argues, is the expression of individual human psychology projected onto a broader stage. The security needs of the ego, are paramount, but the ego is capable of self-deception, of inflation and of an expansionist, imperialistic agenda—whether it is clearing away nature to build another urban tract, reaching for the stars or even conceiving of death as the enemy and conducting "heroic measures" against it.

This hubristic character of the ego may be called the Faust complex,

---

[19] *The Oxford Dictionary of Quotations*, p. 88.

after Goethe's protagonist who on the one hand is noble for his infinite aspirations, but who yet cannot help but reach beyond his capacity to understand and to control consequences. Faust's descendants have made the modern world with all its wonders and all its horrors. Zoja suggests that we carry guilt for each movement away from our natural state, a guilt which troubles sleep and makes the modern dis-eased. As Rilke observed at the beginning of the twentieth century, "We are not much at home / in the world we have created."[20] Thus the march of progress, as it is so frequently called, is the hubristic advance which is paid for with those feelings of dis-ease which constitute existential guilt.

We cannot avoid the experience of well-intentioned choices sometimes having evil consequences, so guilt is a ubiquitous facet of modern life. The Judeo-Christian concept of "sin" (from the Hebrew word meaning "to miss the mark," as in archery) is analogous to the dialectic of hubris-nemesis. Unavoidable to a flawed condition, the individual must still bear the weight of guilt. To understand the inevitability of this *hamartia,* this hubris, this sin, requires the enlargement of consciousness. To know oneself unavoidably flawed, inevitably unconscious, is the first step toward self-acceptance.

Perhaps this existential guilt is the most difficult to bear. To know oneself responsible, not only for the things done, but for the many undone, may broaden one's humanity but it also deepens the pain. In *Tracking the Gods* I describe how such writers as Dostoyevsky, Conrad and Camus depicted the dilemma of the modern who, stunned to consciousness, could only stand shamefaced before the world he or she had chosen. Such an encounter with guilt is ironic. Unlike the tragic sense of life, or the comic vision, the knowledge of the ironic sensibility cannot heal. The ironic consciousness can see the flawed choices, can understand their consequences, but this knowledge is neither redemptive nor avoidable. Such a person is always left with a troubled consciousness, but at least, as Jung pointed out, he or she is thereby less likely to contribute to the burdens of society.

How often we are obliged to face our own bad faith. It is not that we

---

[20] *Duino Elegies,* no. 1, lines 11-12.

are guilty for being neurotic or self-absorbed, but being neurotic or self-absorbed, and knowing it, we have lacked the courage or will to change ourselves. Just as psyche knows when the wounding of life deters or deflects the desire of psyche, so, too, it knows, and registers somewhere, when we live in bad faith with ourselves. And who does not? And who does not, in some deep place, know that? And who does not continue the bad faith? This is existential guilt from which there is no escape, only denial or a deepened acknowledgment.

Given the recognition of our complicity in the evil of the world, and the evil we do ourselves, perhaps self-forgiveness is the hardest goal of all. Inescapably, the first half of life is lived amid the massive unconsciousness of youth; but central to the suffering which arrives at midlife is a necessary accounting of what we have done to others and to ourselves. Learning to forgive oneself is critical but most difficult. The forgiven self is freer to move forward, armed with the enhancement of consciousness which makes life so much richer. But such forgiveness of self, with sincere contrition, symbolic recompense and then release, is rare. Most of us do not achieve personal forgiveness, and the elan of the second half of life is seriously eroded by the adhering consequences of the first. How difficult, but how necessary, it is to internalize Paul Tillich's definition of grace: "Accept the fact that you are accepted, despite the fact that you are unacceptable."[21] Such amazing grace, such release of soul to move deeper into the world.

There is yet another form of existential guilt which constricts the soul. In order to develop as a person, it is sometimes necessary to cross lines once thought too formidable. Every child, to become an adult, must sometimes transgress the parent's will. No parent can ultimately or always know what is right for any child, so the child must leave home, both literally and figuratively. In the not-so-distant past it was commonplace for children to be admonished for not staying with and taking care of their parents. Those who did, at the cost of their own individuation, often grew bitter and depressed. Others, breaking free, still feeling guilty, as if something is owed to the parent, consciously or unconsciously lim-

---

[21] *The Shaking of the Foundations*, p. 162.

ited themselves to the level of psychological development achieved by the parent.

Similarly, a person must sometimes break a commitment in order to grow. Many have stayed in the most abusive of relationships because of what they call guilt, unable to understand that they, too, have a calling to their own separate journey. Sometimes one must even become what in myth is called the Holy Criminal, one who violates the societal norm on behalf of a personal vision. Such a person is obliged to live out this calling even while bearing the burden of consequences as guilt. The conscientious objector is one example. History may forgive the transgressor, but society seldom does, and often the individual cannot either.

As guilt binds us to the past, so it contaminates the present and the future, even unto destruction. For us to deal with guilt in a conscious way we must be able to differentiate the kind of guilt we are suffering. Real guilt is a mature way of taking responsibility. Not only is the flight from that responsibility regressive in character, it means than one can never move beyond the experience which has not been integrated. A friend of my once said, "Guilt butters no parsnips." I suspect she meant that the good energy for life is wasted on the past, and is diverted from the practical assessment of new directions. Only through integration may the necessary consciousness be available to allow new patterns to unfold.

The mature integration of guilt requires the recognition of wrong choices, for which the compensation will often be symbolic rather than literal, and the capacity to let go. Guilt that is inauthentic is a highly repetitive, highly rationalized defense against an unacceptable level of angst. In most cases, the quantity and the quality of that angst marks it as deriving from early childhood experience where the impact of life was all too often more than the child could understand, evaluate and integrate. When one can smoke out the underlying anxiety, then one can often recover the position of conscious and free choice in the present.

The hardest guilt to carry, and perhaps the least resolvable, is existential guilt. Anyone who has attained a measure of consciousness and moral maturity must see the moral thicket through which we wander. We can make no choice, even not to choose, which does not ripple down the line and have a hurtful impact on another, somewhere, somehow. To acknowledge this web of moral interstices is to be caught in the ambiguity of the human condition. To live without hubris or sin or self-delusion is equally impossible. From such crossing of the invisible lines, counter-forces are set in motion which surge back upon our shores. We need to meditate on the irony of life, to realize, like St. Paul, that though we would do good we do not, that we are our own worst enemy, and that much of what we do is to flee our fuller selves and thereby remain stuck.

Such knowledge may not bring release, but it is the mark of a mature person who, having differentiated the permutations of guilt, has at least a chance to achieve a measure of release from the bonds of the past. The energy reclaimed in the process can be reinvested in an enlarged future.

Yet, for most of us, Ilse seems the prototype of our own troubled transit. She wanders the guilty planet seeking release from the past, and from herself. I sincerely hope she will find at last one of the Just and know release. I, too, now carry her secret. And sometimes, too, I can sense my arm around one child as I pull on the other, the one with the bruised knee whose hand clings to mine and whose fearful transit never ends.

2
Grief, Loss and Betrayal

What Is Desired May Not Be Held

Devin is now thirty-eight. His father was an architect, his brother is an architect, and Devin trained to be and for a while practiced as an architect. He came to be so blessed by grief, loss and betrayal that he found the soul he did not know he had lost.

Devin's father had been a kindly yet controlling man, an alcoholic patriarch, giving love and expecting loyalty. Devin knew clearly what he was supposed to do when he grew up: become an architect, live in the immediate neighborhood and stay loyal to his family. His older brother followed those instructions exactly, and Devin set off on "the first adulthood," the one where the phenomenological experiences of childhood are internalized as a set of perceptions of self and others, for which the child develops reflexive strategies for managing anxiety.[22]

Devin not only became an architect, he also married and settled down in the same neighborhood, reporting to the family as expected. His mother had colluded with the system in typically co-dependent ways. After her husband's death, Devin was immediately promoted to be his mother's emotional caretaker.

At first glance Devin's wife, Anne, seemed quite different from his family. She was an intellectual, a writer, avant garde in her political views and life style, but she also turned out to be alcoholic and emotionally unstable. In her thirties she contracted cancer, and Devin devoted himself to her faithfully until her death. For two years he was emotionally disabled by the loss. Their life together had been turbulent, tragic and traumatic, but Devin was nothing if not loyal, and programmed from childhood to be the caretaker of the wounded family. He knew who he was by his job definition. In so many such families, one child is nomi-

---

[22] See my book, *The Middle Passage: From Misery to Meaning in Midlife,* pp. 9ff., for an account of how one unavoidably acquires a false or provisional self and sets off into adulthood in wounded and self-estranging ways.

nated, by a silent council which transpires in the collusive unconscious-ness of the parents, to be keeper of the flame, scapegoat and caretaker of the walking wounded. Devin had silently accepted his nomination and carried out his assigned tasks well.

Devin came to therapy because of a psychic numbness, a mythological disorientation. His wife was dead. He could no longer go to the architec-tural firm and draw plans for better living. He no longer knew who he was or what he wanted to do with his life. Toward the end of the two years, and around the time of beginning therapy, he began dating again. Denise was a woman he had known many years before but left in order to pursue the relationship with Anne. During the interim years Denise had not married, had pursued a professional career, and had become emotionally and economically self-sufficient. When Devin spoke of the renewed relationship with Denise, he spoke of her with affection but be-lieved there could be no committed future together. He did not know why. While he admired Denise, even loved her, he could not see himself in relationship again.

It was easy enough to diagnose Devin's condition as a reactive depres-sion. But because it lasted beyond a year after his wife's death and per-meated his life so extensively, I surmised that the depression was only the tip of a much deeper malaise and disaffection. Devin had arrived at a turning point in his life, a "middle passage" between the false self, gen-erated by the internalized precepts of his family of origin, and the person he was meant to become.

Whenever one goes through the deconstruction of the false self, one normally suffers a considerable period of disorientation, of wandering in the wasteland. "Wandering between two worlds," as Matthew Arnold de-scribed, "One dead, one powerless to be born."[23] No career, no rela-tionship, no direction or desire emerges, for one is absent-spirited, adrift, without vision of a renewed sense of self. Nothing meant anything to Devin during this time for everything was contaminated by its locus in the economy of the false self. Only reading and the love of music and na-ture stirred the currents of his soul.

---

[23] "Stanzas from 'The Grand Chartreuse,' " in *Poetry and Criticism of Matthew Arnold*, p. 187.

As we worked in therapy, chipping away at the old self, which simply did not work anymore, it was easy to slip into trying to engineer the future. But any such future would be organized by ego consciousness, not derived from a deep place in the personality. So there was great resistance, a torpor which resembled lassitude, even laziness, but was in fact a resistance to a false journey. Perhaps the critical turn in the therapy occurred when Devin brought Denise into therapy with him in order to explain to her his seeming recalcitrance, a resistance to her which she could only experience as a personal rejection. In the course of our hour together Denise happened to mention her relation to Devin's mother. The mother was very friendly to her, but at the same time she took every opportunity to denigrate her own son. "The only thing he is really good for," the mother said, "is getting the house real clean."

Denise also pointed out how Devin's siblings called on him at the last moment, to babysit, pick them up at the airport, help them with house maintenance and so on, and how Devin, *semper fideles*, always obliged. The picture that emerged was of a gifted, intelligent man still very much imprisoned by his family of origin. His mother knew enough to mollify her son's girlfriend, but also sought to sabotage the relationship so that she could maintain exclusive rights to her child. The siblings also assumed Devin's role in the family structure and took advantage of him reflexively.

What was oppressing Devin so profoundly, albeit unconsciously, was not the loss of his wife as much as the loss of his own self through the years of constant demands and expectations. Through the conversation with Denise, Devin began to understand the exploitative nature of his familial enmeshment. Then life stirred within him and the Angel of Desire could once again be seen. (Etymologically, the word "desire" comes from the Latin *de* and *sidus*, "to have lost one's navigational star.") As C. Day-Lewis wrote,

> Move then with new desires,
> For where we used to build and love
> Is no-man's land, and only ghosts can live
> Between two fires.[24]

---

[24] "The Conflict," in *Modern American and British Poetry,* p. 597.

Two weeks later Devin had the following dream.

I am going to an Elvis Presley concert at the Spectrum. Since I am going to see Elvis, the way I combed my hair is very important. Elvis is on-stage singing. He is very young and is singing one of my favorite songs. To the left of the stage is a screen behind which a naked woman is taking a bath. She steps out of the tub and as she does Elvis catches my eye and gives me a knowing look. There is nothing leering in his look. Rather, her presence seems to give Elvis strength, power and wholeness. She was part of the show but only for me to see.

As I walk out of the Spectrum I see Anne standing there. She gives me a Bible, but it is not the Christian Bible. Anne says, "She's at it again," and I realize that it is a Bible written and painted by her sister Rose during her schizophrenic periods. The cover is a painting of the Apocalypse.

I ask Anne what I am to do with this and she says, "I want you to edit it and put it in shape." I feel torn. I love her but am reluctant to accept the book because it comes from everything bad in our relationship—the evil influence of our families, my role in making sense of everyone else's confusion, and my need to save Anne from the world and herself.

I realize that Anne is drunk again. I realize that she lives off of the sadness she absorbs from life. I tell her that I am going to marry Denise, but not to hurt her. Then she says, "Everyone thought we were dumb together." Then she says, "How 'bout them Phils? Them Iggs?" I understand then that our life was stupid and superficial. We spent too much time living in false feelings, never examining what was important to us. I realize that we will never be together again, and that saddens me, but I will marry Denise, and Anne will continue in sadness and solitude because, for her, there is no other way.

This dream demonstrates the enormous autonomous forces at work in Devin's psyche, forces seeking rebirth from a living death. While he seems to have been immobilized by the loss of his wife, in fact his psyche was in profound revolt. His loss became the catalyst for the reexamination of his own life. To understand the depth of this experience one has to understand that his greatest loss had been the loss of his own psychic integrity, the grief not so much for his wife as for his lost soul.

One of the ways in which Devin was able to move to a new sense of self was to appreciate the gift of the dream, the extraordinary commentary which his own psyche had provided to help him understand the past, free himself from it and move on.

In Devin's associations to the above dream, Elvis suggested a "mana personality," a charismatic singer of the soul when Devin had known so little song in his duty-bound life. The naked woman on stage, meant only for him to see, suggested a bolder recognition of the anima. Before he could consider a new relationship, he had to bring the phenomenal energies of Elvis together with the noumenal energies of the anima, the Angel of Desire which animates life.

When Anne hands Devin the Bible, it implies not only the duty-bound admonitions of his youth, but also the madness he found in his wife's family. Her sister Rose had in fact been psychotic and Devin had played the central part in the caretaking. His job, in the dream as in life, was to edit and put things into shape for those who were unable or unwilling to do it for themselves. But in the dream Devin is able to see what he had not previously known consciously, that he no longer belongs in that sorry world, making other people's lives work, saving them from themselves.

Now he sees Anne not only as the needy person he was trained to protect, but as diversionary and superficial—she deflects their profound encounter into a discussion of the Phillies and Eagles sports teams. Devin sees with the clarity of an ancient Greek tragedy that he has lived in a sham world, and, saddened by the loss, the stuckness, the grief for those left behind in the underworld, he prepares to give himself to the new land, the new relationship, the new sense of self. Two weeks after the dream Devin and Denise became engaged.

Only great loss could have provided the catalyst to encounter another loss which lay so deeply as to be unconscious—the loss of his own journey. Only grief could stir him to finally face his estrangement from himself. And only the betrayal of Anne could have led him to see the exploitative nature of his family relationships.

By dwelling in these dismal swamplands, and working through their grievous woundings, Devin recovered the life he was always meant to have—his own, not someone else's. Out of the depths of loss, grief and betrayal he recovered his desire, his own star.

Loss and Grief

Next to existential angst, perhaps no experience is more recurrent in our troubled transit than loss. Our life begins with loss. We are profoundly separated from the protective womb, disconnected from the heartbeat of the cosmos, thrust into an uncertain and often murderous world. This birth trauma marks the beginning of the journey which ends with the loss of life itself. Along the way there are repeated losses—of security, of connectedness, of unconsciousness, of innocence, and progressively, the loss of comrades, bodily energies and stages of ego identification. It is no wonder that all cultures have mythologies that dramatize this sense of loss and disconnection—myths of the Fall, the primal separation from the presumed Edenic state, the Golden Age, the memory of unity with nature and the mother. Similarly, all peoples exhibit a profound nostalgia for that connectedness.

The theme of loss runs through our culture from the most maudlin of song lyrics, wherein we hear the lament that life has lost its meaning because of the absence of the beloved, to most anguished, yearning prayers of the mystics for union with God. For Dante, the greatest of pains was the loss of hope, the loss of salvation, the loss of paradise, and to be haunted by the memory of the promise of connection, a promise which itself is now lost. Loss is central to our condition. If we live long enough, we will lose everyone for whom we care. If we do not live long enough, they will have lost us. As Rilke puts it, "So we live, forever saying farewell."[25] The "farewell" is to people, to states of being, to the departing moment. Elsewhere Rilke personifies parting: "Parting, with her fingers poised at her lips."[26] The German word for loss, *Verlust,* suggests "going through desire" to experience, then, the absence of its object. Beyond the desire, always, is the loss.

Twenty-five hundred years ago Gautama became the Buddha (one who "sees through"). What he saw was that life is the permanent experience of suffering. This suffering is primarily occasioned by the ego's desire to control—to control the environment, to control others, to control even mortality. Since we are unable to successfully control life, we suffer in proportion to our losses. The only path through and beyond this suffering, according to the Buddha, is the relinquishment of the desire to control, to let be, to go with the wisdom implicit in the transience of nature.

---

[25] *Duino Elegies,* no. 8, line 75.
[26] Ibid., no. 4, line 101.

This release is the proper cure for neurosis, for then one is not split off from nature, including ourselves, who are a part of nature.

Such a relinquishment does not render one a slave to loss, but rather a participant in the act of letting go. Only letting go can bring peace and serenity. But, as we all know, the ego's prime officer is Captain Security, ably supported by Sergeant Control. Who among us has "seen through" like the Buddha and has extinguished desire, transcended the ego and affirmed with the heart the idea of "not my will but Thine"? We are told by Tennyson that it is better to have loved and lost than not to have loved at all. The day after the assassination of John Kennedy, his relative Kenny O'Donnell said on the radio, "What's the use of being Irish if you don't know that sooner or later the world will break your heart?"

The Buddha's wise counsel notwithstanding, it seems of our nature to long for attachment, for home. Somewhere, in the collision between heart, which longs for permanency and connection, and brain, which acknowledges separation and loss, there is a place for us to find our personal psychology. None of us will likely attain Buddhahood, but we need not be eternal victims either.

Central to the enlargement of consciousness is the acknowledgment that the constancy of life is its impermanence. Indeed, transiency is the expression of the life force itself. As Dylan Thomas expressed the paradox, "The force that through the green fuse drives the flower is my destroyer."[27] The same energy that ignites natural energy, like the fuse of a stick of dynamite, feeds on itself and is consumed. Such evanescence is itself life. The word we have for that which is unchanging is *death*. The embrace of life, thus, requires the embrace of that energy which feeds on itself and is consumed. Not to change is contrary to the life force, is death.

This is why Wallace Stevens concluded that "Death is the mother of beauty,"[28] and that death was nature's greatest invention. Along with the experience of the force that consumes itself comes the capacity for consciousness, meaningful choice and an appreciation of beauty. There is a wisdom here that transcends the bounds and anxieties of the ego, a wis-

---

[27] "The Force That Through the Green Fuse," in *Norton Anthology of Poetry,* p. 1176.
[28] "Sunday Morning," in ibid., p. 931.

dom that embodies the secret unity of life and death, attachment and loss, as being part of the same great round.[29] Such wisdom confronts the ego's need and lifts it out of the petty into the transcendent.

The secret unity of attachment and loss, holding and losing, is wonderfully expressed in Rilke's poem appropriately titled "Autumn," that season which we in the northern hemisphere associate with the loss of summer and the onset of winter's losses. The poem ends:

> All of us are falling. See this hand now fall.
> And now see the others; it is part of all.
>
> And still there is one who in his hands gently
> Holds this falling endlessly.[30]

Rilke enlarges the falling leaves into the earth falling through space and time, into the experience of loss and fall as universal, and intimates that there is a secret unity underneath the falling which sustains it. If this is God, Rilke does not say so; he contents himself in that great round of attachment and loss, which seem disparate but are somehow aspects of the same thing.

The experience of loss can only be acute when something of value has been in our life. If there is no experience of loss, there was nothing of value. To suffer loss we are required to acknowledge the value we have been granted. Freud wrote an essay titled "Mourning and Melancholy" in which he observed that the child who loses a parent through death can grieve a loss and therefore release some of its energy. The child whose parent is physically present but emotionally absent cannot grieve, for the parent is not, literally, gone. This frustrated grieving is then internalized as melancholy, the sadness of loss and the yearning for reconnection, a yearning in direct proportion to its value for the child. Thus, the experience of loss can only come after the value has been part of our lives. The task in this swampland of suffering is to discern the value we have been granted and to hold it even when we cannot hold to what concretely gave rise to it.

---

[29] See my *Tracking the Gods,* pp. 54ff., for a discussion of the mythologem of the Great Round, the Eternal Return, the Cycle of Sacrifice.

[30] In Flores, trans. and ed., *An Anthology of German Poetry,* p. 390.

When we lose a loved one, we need to grieve that loss and yet consciously value what we have internalized from that person. The parent who suffers the empty nest syndrome, for example, suffers less the loss of the child than the implicit identity which went with being that child's parent. The energy invested in that role is now available for a different direction. So, we honor best those we have lost by making their contribution to our lives conscious, living with that value deliberately, and incorporating that value in the on-going life enterprise. This is the proper conversion of inescapable loss into this evanescent life. Such conversion is not denial but transformation. Nothing which is internalized is ever lost. Even in loss, then, something soulful remains.

The word "grief" derives from the Latin *gravis,* "to bear," and from which we get our word "gravity." To experience grief is not only to bear the heaviness of the condition but, again, to testify to depth as well. We only grieve what has value. Surely one of the deepest pains of grief is the sense of impotence, the reminder of how little we are in control of life. As Cicero observed, "It is foolish to tear one's hair in grief, as though sorrow would be made less by baldness."[31] And yet we sympathize with Zorba the Greek, who scandalized his village when, having lost his daughter, he danced all night because he could only express through the body the corybanthine excess of his loss. Grief, like other primal emotions, resists words, resists being pinned down and analyzed.

Arguably the most profound poem on grief was written in the nineteenth century by Dante Gabriel Rossetti, called "The Woodspurge." The word "grief" is only mentioned once, in the final stanza. Rather one senses the speaker's disorientation, loose ends, a profound disconnection. All he seems capable of is describing in detail the intricacies of the flowering woodspurge. The gravity of grief looms so large that it is beyond comprehension; he can only focus on the finite details of nature.

> From perfect grief there need not be
> Wisdom or even memory;
> One thing then learnt remains to me—
> The woodspurge has a cup of three.[32]

---

[31] *The Oxford Dictionary of Quotations,* p. 151.
[32] *Norton Anthology of Poetry,* p. 798.

Rossetti understands how unapproachable is great loss and so, like Rilke in employing the metaphor of autumnal falling, intimates the infinite through the knowable finite. Again, from the honesty of grief comes the acknowledgment of the value once held. In the Jewish faith the "unveiling" of the grave stone on the first anniversary is a dual acknowledgment of the gravity of loss and a reminder of the end of grieving so that life might renew itself.

No amount of denial will spare us loss. Nor should we hesitate to grieve. Midway between the fretting of the heart and the fevers of the brain is the chance to accept the evanescence of things, our poor power to hold on, and yet to affirm what has been, if only briefly, ours. At the conclusion of Archibald MacLeish's reworking of the Job story, *J.B.*, J.B. says of God, "He does not love, He Is." "But we do," says Sarah, his wife. "That's the wonder."[33] The power to affirm value amid loss is a source of deep meaning. Holding to the meaning and letting go of control is the double work of loss and grief.

When Jung's wife Emma died, he suffered a reactive depression. For months he was bereft and disoriented. Then one night he dreamt that he had entered a theater where he was alone. He went down to the front row and waited. An orchestra pit loomed like an abyss before him. When the curtain opened, he saw Emma standing there, in white dress, smiling at him, and he knew the silence was broken. They were together, whether together or apart.

As I planned my first return to the Jung Institute in Zürich after three years practicing in the States, I looked forward to seeing many old friends, most notably Dr. Adolph Ammann, who had been my supervising analyst. Just before returning I learned that he had died and I grieved the loss and disconnection. Then, at 3 a.m., November 4, 1985, I "woke up" to see Dr. Ammann in my bedroom. He smiled, bowed in his familiar courtly way, and said, "Good to see you again." I thought three things: "This is no dream—he is really here"; then, "This must, surely, be a dream"; and then, "This is like Jung's dream of Emma. I have not lost him for he is still here with me." So the experience ended with a deep

---

[33] *J.B.*, p. 152.

sense of peace and acceptance. I had not lost my friend-mentor because he is still within, even as I write these words.

Perhaps nothing which was ever real, which was ever important, which ever had gravity, is ever really lost. Only in the letting go of the fantasy of control can one truly grieve loss, truly celebrate value.

Betrayal

Betrayal is a form of loss as well. What is lost is innocence, trust and simple relationship. All of us suffer betrayal at times, even on the cosmic level. The assumptions of the ego, the private fantasies of omnipotence, sustain heavy blows. (Nietzsche noted how disappointed we were the day we discerned we were not God.)

The discrepancy between ego fantasies and the limitations of our fragile lives often seems part of a cosmic betrayal, as if some universal parent had let us down. As Frost so wittily noted, "Lord, forgive my little joke on thee / And I'll forgive Thy great big joke on me."[34] And Jesus on the cross cries, "My God, my God . . . why hast Thou forsaken me?"

We naturally want protection from the worrisome world, from ambivalence and ambiguity, and we project the child's need for the protective parent onto the indifferent universe. The child's expectation for protection and love is often betrayed. Even in the most benign of households, the twin woundings of overwhelment or abandonment are inevitable. Perhaps nothing so chills a parent's heart as the realization that just by being ourselves we wound our children. So, every child feels betrayed by the humanness, the limitations, of the parent—some more than others. Aldo Carotenuto notes,

> We can only be deceived by those we trust. Yet we have to believe. A person who won't have faith and refuses to love for fear of betrayal will certainly be exempt from these torments, but who knows from how much else he or she will be exempt?[35]

The greater this "betrayal" of innocence, trust and faith, the more likely the child will grow to distrust the world. The experience of profound betrayal leads to a paranoia, a transferential universalization of

---

[34] "Forgive," in *Robert Frost's Poems*, p. 261.
[35] *Eros and Pathos: Shades of Love and Suffering*, p. 79.

loss. One man whom I saw briefly recalled the day when his mother walked away from him forever. While in a loving and devoted marriage, he could never trust his wife, followed her everywhere, insisted that she undergo polygraph tests to affirm her loyalty, and saw in the smallest of incidents evidence of betrayal, which he thought his fate. Despite her repeated assurances of loyalty, he finally drove her away from him, seeing in her departure confirmation of what he had always believed, that he had been betrayed once and forever.

Indeed, paranoid thoughts lurk in all of us in some measure, for we have all been wounded by the cosmos, by the existential condition, and by those in whom we have placed trust.

Trust and betrayal are necessary opposites. If one has been betrayed—and who has not—how difficult it is then to trust. Often when the child has been deeply betrayed through the neglect or abuse of the parent, he or she later bonds with someone who will repeat the betrayal—a pattern called "reaction formation," or a "self-fulfilling prophecy"—or avoids intimacy in the hope of avoiding the hurt again. In either strategy, the legacy of the past wound dominates choices in the present. One is still defined, as in the case of guilt, by the past. Yet to be in relationship, to invest in it trustfully, is to presuppose the capacity for betrayal as well. If we do not trust, then we are not invested at the depth that makes intimacy possible. If we do not invest at this risk-laden depth, then genuine intimacy is precluded. The paradox of the trust/betrayal dyad, then, is that each is presupposed by the other. Without trust, no depth; without depth, no true betrayal.

As we noted of guilt, it is most difficult to forgive betrayal, especially that which seems deliberate. Yet the capacity to forgive is not only an implicit recognition of our own capacity to betray, it is the only move which can free us from the shackles of the past. How often do we see embittered souls, still unforgiving of the former spouse who betrayed them? They are, through their enslavement to the past, still married to the betrayer, still defined and corroded by the acid of hate. I have also seen divorced persons who carry a hatred of former spouses not for what they did, but for what they did not do.

Julianne was a Daddy's Girl. She found a man who would take care of her. While she chafed at his guidance, and he at her neediness, both were defined by this unconscious contract, that he would be her husband-father and she his devoted daughter. When her husband outgrew this unconscious bargain, struck when both were in their earlier twenties, she was infuriated. She remained girlish and petulant, unaware that her husband's departure was her wake-up call to adulthood. His betrayal of her seemed total, unforgivable, when what she was really betrayed by was the parent-child fusion from which she had never separated. Suffice to say, she quickly found another man with whom to play out the old dependency. The invitation to grow up was refused.

Betrayal is often experienced as an isolation of self. The other upon whom one counted, or of whom one had certain expectations, or with whom one played out an unconscious *folie à deux* is now suspect and one's fundamental assumptions are shaken. In such an altered state, considerable growth is possible. We can learn from our wounds, but if we do not, we will repeat them in another forum or identify ourselves with them. Many stay stuck in the past thus, "wound-identified." God seems to "betray" Job, but in the end Job's casual assumptions about the universe are shaken; he moves to a new level of consciousness and converts his ordeal to a blessing from that God. Jesus feels betrayed not only by Judas, but by his Father, and yet in his final acceptance achieves the epiphanic consummation at Golgotha.

Naturally we feel outraged with betrayal and are likely to pursue revenge. But revenge not only constricts rather than enlarges consciousness, but, again, binds us to the past. Those consumed by revenge, however legitimate their grievance, remain forever victims. They are still back at the original betrayal, and all the life which could have been theirs since has been thwarted. Similarly, one may, through various forms of denial, choose to remain unconscious. This ploy, which is a refusal to feel the hurt one already suffers, is a resistance to the growth obliged by any lost Eden, any demand for enlarged consciousness.

The third temptation of the betrayed is to generalize the experience, as in the paranoia of the man whose mother abandoned him. If she left him, surely any other woman for whom he cared would as well. This paranoia, understandable as it may seem from within the frame of that experience, becomes a contaminating cynicism about all relationships. The tendency to generalize from an acute experience of betrayal keeps one on the continuum ranging from suspicion and avoidance of intimacy to paranoia and scapegoating.

Betrayal stings us toward individuation. If the betrayal is of our existential naiveté, we are driven toward the embrace of the greater wisdom of the universe whose dialectic seems to be attachment and loss; if the betrayal is of our dependency, we are driven to face where we long to remain infantile; if the betrayal is of one conscious being toward another, we are driven to suffer and embrace the polarities which are found not only in the betrayer but in ourselves as well. In every case, if we do not remain behind, stuck in recriminations, we are enlarged, more complex, more conscious. Carotenuto has summarized this dilemma well:

> The experience of betrayal, translated into psychological terms, provides the opportunity to experience one of the fundamental processes of psychic life, the integration of ambivalence, including the love-hate feelings that exist in every relationship. It must be emphasized again that this experience does not involve only the one who usually takes the blame, but also the betrayed, who unconsciously set in motion the events that led to betrayal.[36]

The most bitter pill in betrayal, then, may be our grudging recognition, often years later, that we ourselves were part of the collusive ballet which led in time to betrayal. If we can swallow such a bitter pill, we will have a much larger sense of our shadow. We will not always like what we are summoned to acknowledge. Again, as Jung said, "The experience of the Self is always a defeat for the ego."[37] In describing his own descent into his unconscious in the second decade of this century, Jung tells how he was forced, repeatedly, to say, "Here is another thing you did not know about yourself."[38] But from such a bitter herb does much consciousness evolve.

Through the suffering of loss, grief and betrayal we are pulled down and under, and possibly through, to a larger Weltanschauung. Devin, for

---

[36] Ibid., p. 81.
[37] *Mysterium Coniunctionis*, CW 14, par. 778.
[38] *Memories, Dreams, Reflections*, p. 183.

instance, seemed stuck in the morass of grief for his deceased wife. But the desuetude and disorientation of that time was disproportionate to his loss. By working through the experience, he came to see that he himself was lost, grieving for his unlived life, betrayed since childhood into living someone else's plan. Only by suffering through those terrible two years could he come at last to the start of his own journey.

The message of loss and grief and betrayal is that we cannot hold on to anything, cannot take anything or anyone for granted, cannot spare ourselves acute pain. But what abides is the invitation to consciousness. What is constant amid inconstancy is the summons to individuation. We are neither our point of origin nor our goal; the former is long gone, the latter forever recedes as we move forward. We are the journey itself. Loss, grief and betrayal are not just dismal places we must unwillingly visit, they are integral to the maturation of consciousness. They are as much a part of the journey as the places where we feel respite and would tarry. The great rhythm of gain and loss is outside of our control; what remains within our control is the attitude of willingness to find in even the bitterest losses what remains to be lived.

3
Doubt and Loneliness

l(a

le
af
fa

ll

s)
one
l

iness

—e.e. cummings.

The Silence of Infinite Spaces

In his *Pensées*, the French mathematician-mystic Blaise Pascal wrote, "The silence of these infinite spaces frightens me."[39] Who has not awakened at four in the morning and felt horribly alone, vulnerable and afraid? Who has not experienced the silence of the infinite spaces without and the infinite spaces within? Who has not intimated in the leaf's fall the evanescence of things human and one's aloneness on the planet, as e.e. cummings's poem so starkly illustrates? Or, as Robert Frost expressed it,

> They cannot scare me with their empty spaces
> Between stars—on stars where no human race is.
> I have it in me so much nearer home
> To scare myself with my own desert places.[40]

Who has not felt insufficient to meet the demands of life, and wished for some deliverance? Who has not watched the familiar slip away and felt thrown back solely on one's own meager resources?

---

[39] *Pensées*, no. 206, p. 61.
[40] "Desert Places," in Richard Ellmann and Robert O'Clair, eds., *Modern Poems*, p. 80.

> . . . even the comforting barn grows far away.
> And my heart owns a doubt
> Whether 'tis in us to arise with day
> And save ourselves unaided.[41]

In each of these swampland states there is a developmental task. Just as Jung suggested that in each therapy one should ask what task this person is avoiding through his or her neurosis, so we have to ask what task is implicit in each of these dismal places. In every case it is some variant of gaining permission, leaving a dependency or finding the courage to stand vulnerably and responsibly before the universe. In every case we are challenged to grow up, to take on the journey with greater consciousness. While such enlargement is often terrifying, it is also freeing and brings dignity and meaning to our lives.

Norman had had two marriages by the time he was thirty. In each he had stormed his intended's citadel with flattery, pseudosophistication, charm and cajolery. Shortly after each marriage he burst into rage when his bride did not attend his needs; he controlled her mobility and choices, and launched verbal attacks which led to physical abuse. When she proved intractable, Norman divorced her and set off to find the next.

The second wife managed to shoe-horn Norman into a brief marital therapy, during which time he alternately raged, threatened and bullied. He refused to discuss his own background or to acknowledge that he might play a significant role in the distresses of the current marriage. The therapist was soon obliged to terminate the therapy, for it could not go forward without each party's willingness to own their own patterns and responsibilities.

When one looks at Norman's life there is a clear pattern. Driven to connect with the feminine, as soon as she draws close he abuses her. The very deep split in his psyche which this represents, needing and fearing at the same time, can only derive from some primal experience such as Norman's relationship with his mother.

What Norman cannot abide is doubt; he must have guarantees. Like a fundamentalist who is so fearful of ambiguity that he or she must insist

---

[41] Robert Frost, "Storm Fear," in *Robert Frost's Poems,* p. 245.

on a rigid truth, and even oppresses a neighbor who differs, Norman cannot risk looking within, cannot risk doubting the great lie which constitutes his provisional sense of self. The child who was abused by the mother still needs her; at the same time he fears and hates her. The earlier in his development this trauma occurs, the more systemic his defenses will be, the more pervasive his transference of those dynamics onto others, and the more untouchable the unhealed wound. Thus, he will, like all those with a characterological disorder, spend his life wounding others in return, incapable of reflection and psychological responsibility.

It could be said that the neurotic, and that includes most of us, is his or her own worst enemy—racked with guilt and a sense of failure, haunted by inadequacies. The characterological disorder derives from wounds so early, so devastating, that the individual lacks sufficient ego strength to dialogue with personal materials. The affects attending their issues are too powerfully charged to confront and so they are pushed into the unconscious, and often projected onto others. While such a person may hold a position of power in the society, he or she is forever trapped in childhood. The primal wounding defines and directs each decision and will continue to poison relationships precisely because the person is too weak to tolerate the doubt which is the necessary precursor to growth and the transcendence of that early wound.

Norman's life is fed by a deep underground spring of wounding and desire. Like any child, he longs for Mother's solicitude, but his mother betrayed her role and forever charged that feminine imago in Norman with fear sufficient to match the desire. Thus he desperately seeks connection with "Her," and at the same time fears her. As one only attacks what one fears, so his fear is very great indeed. But it is also his secret, a secret he must keep from himself. Such secrets are toxic; they invariably spill over into relationships and wound others. Until Norman can consciously suffer the anguish of self-doubt, he will unconsciously stay frozen in his history.

Given the fact that the top priority of the ego is security, doubt is an unwelcome visitor to us. Fortunately, most of us are not as wounded as Norman and can admit to doubt. At times we may even be overwhelmed and paralyzed by it. The German word for doubt, *Zweifeln* ("twoness"), suggests the split we feel when we experience doubt. How to admit doubt, which is the precursor for all growth, without being overwhelmed and paralyzed by it, is no small task.

The ego is like a petty tyrant who must fulminate on the rightness of its position as a compensation for the swamp of doubt upon which its castle is built. Tennyson noted, "There lives more faith in honest doubt, / Believe me, than in half the creeds."[42] And Wilson Mizner echoed, "I respect faith. But doubt is what gets you an education."[43] The position which is intractable, which cannot reflect on itself, which cannot critique itself, is fascistic, monolithic, stuck. "Loyalty to petrified opinion," observed Goethe, "never yet broke a chain, or freed a human soul."[44] Such petrified opinion can be a political or religious dogma, or, closer to home, our own reified sense of self. With doubt, of course, comes greater angst, hence the many defenses mounted against it. Risking doubt means risking greater anxiety. But to risk greater anxiety is to open to the enlargement of personality against which our rigid standpoint is a defense.

What good can be said of doubt, good which even the nervous ego might accept? Actually, many things.

Doubt is the necessary fuel for change, and therefore growth. There is no scientific or theological dogma which does not contain within it the seeds of reification and tyranny. Similarly, the psyche summons us, quite apart from the desires of the ego, to relinquish what seemed clear, what protected us, and thereby what now mires us in yesterday. The problem, then, is not doubt; the problem is fear of change. Confronting the risk of doubt is necessary for any group or individual to grow.

Doubt is essential for democracy. Notice how powerful are those forces in any country that wish to define what it means to be an American, a Canadian, a German or whatever. Notice how institutions such as legislatures, courts and social agencies are pressured by the anxious few to adhere to constrictive values and to contain the forces of diversity. The child who points out that the emperor is in fact naked will never be welcomed by the collective. So, too, in our private lives, our typologies,

---

[42] *The Oxford Dictionary of Quotations,* p. 537.
[43] Ibid., p. 352.
[44] Ibid., p. 230.

our neurotic patterns, our repetition compulsion, our rigid outlooks, we reject the discordant, the dialectical, the disaffected.

Jung once noted that individuation does not come from on high, from the royal ego managing affairs, but from "the little people," the split-off energies which are the peasants of the inner kingdom.[45] While the ego would like to make the universe of the soul monocratic and monotheistic, the psyche is in fact polytheistic and powerfully democratic, with many split-off energies or complexes. The enlarged sense of self requires a dialogue with these energies and an ego both open and humble. Most of us have only truly grown when our ego's haughty power was brought down. When our walls were broken, a new perspective became possible. Thus, the doubt which keeps alive the dialectical values, and therefore protects a culture from reification and stagnation, also serves to enliven the personality and stimulate it to evolve.

Doubt is a form of radical faith. The only way we can remain faithful to the mystery of mystery is to preserve ambiguity. Certainty is the enemy of truth. The truly faithful person is the iconoclast who must, from time to time, break the old categories in order to free the energy to flow again. All concepts, whether dogmas or operative beliefs, are husks which once held the energy but which can also serve as a prison. This is what William Blake meant when, surveying the dreariness of London, he lamented most, "the mind-forged manacles of man."[46] The toxicity of such imprisonment is an omnipresent reality for both society and the individual.

No one in modern life has spoken more eloquently about the value of doubt than the theologian Paul Tillich. Our faith, he believed, is not found so much in our conscious beliefs as in the regions of our "ultimate concerns."[47] Thus, he noted, our de facto, daily religiosity might prove less Methodist than mercantile, less Nazarene than neurotic, less Anglican than addictive, and so on. But doubt, Tillich argued, is the necessary ingredient in any respectful encounter with ultimacy. As we cannot know

---

[45] "A Review of the Complex Theory," *The Structure and Dynamics of the Psyche,* CW 8, par. 209.
[46] "London," in *Norton Anthology of Poetry,* p. 506.
[47] *The Dynamics of Faith,* p. 1.

what the ultimate things are, so we are summoned to leave open some part of our view for the divine energy to enter anew. The god which can be named is not God. It is the affectively charged image that arises from the ruin of the broken belief that constitutes the new numinosity. This doubt is a form of humility before the largeness of the mystery. It is a form of honesty. It is a manifestation of how seriously one in fact takes one's journey, an expression of how deeply one cares.

Whether it is our beliefs that must suffer doubt in order to grow, or our certainties about ourselves that must be shattered, doubt is the agency of change and renewal. Doubt overthrows the petty monarch ego whose tyranny enslaves. Norman cannot grow into himself, can never stop hurting those around him, unless he can admit to the lie his conscious sense of self embodies. He is stuck because he cannot doubt himself. The task for each of us, then, remains to risk the increased anxiety of ambiguity which doubt brings, in order to receive the blessing of growth.

Alone on the High Seas of the Soul

Life, consciousness and the fearsome journey of the soul all begin with traumatic separation. Connected to the heartbeat of the cosmos, all needs met in the warm, wet world of the womb, we are suddenly thrust onto a cold, spinning planet falling through space and time. We never recover, nor can we ever fully reexperience our sense of *participation mystique,* our identification, with the universe. How much of an exaggeration is it to say that all of our life is spent trying either to recover that lost connection by some form of regressive impulse or to sublimate this deep need into a search for connection with nature, with others, with the gods?

But the connections are never sustainable nor complete and one feels the angst and anguish of disconnection, of one's aloneness in the cosmos. Even when connection seems to have occurred, one quickly becomes acutely, painfully, apprised of one's isolation anew. Rilke said it well in his poem "Loneliness": though "in one bed [we] sleep together / Loneliness goes on then with the rivers."[48]

Our aloneness is mediated somewhat in childhood by the presence of parents or parent surrogates, and in the first adulthood by the domination

---

[48] In Flores, trans. and ed., *An Anthology of German Poetry,* p. 387.

of the parental complexes and their transference onto others. But even the most functional of relationships can only approximate the original connectedness. Thus by midlife everyone has had to confront the limits of relationship, the limits of socialized roles in a protective society, and the limits of their own powers of denial and transference. The recognition that no one can save us, protect us from death, or even sufficiently distract us, becomes unavoidable. The two greatest fantasies we are obliged to relinquish in the second half of life are that we are immortal exceptions to the human condition, and that out there somewhere is some "magical Other" who will rescue us from existential isolation.

As an analyst, I have found that whether or not a person progresses in therapy, which is to say matures as a human being, is a direct function of one's ability to take responsibility for choices, to cease blaming others or expecting rescue from them, and to acknowledge the pain of loneliness however much one may be invested in social roles and relationships.

Thomas Wolfe describes the ubiquity and importance of the experience of loneliness:

> The whole conviction of my life now rests upon the belief that loneliness, far from being a rare and curious phenomenon . . . is the central and inevitable fact of human existence. . . . All this hideous doubt, despair, and dark confusion of the soul a lonely man must know, for he is united to no image save that which he creates himself. . . . He is sustained and cheered and aided by no party, he is given comfort by no creed, he has no faith in him except his own. And often that faith deserts him, leaving him shaken and filled with impotence.[49]

Wolfe's view is rather bleaker than that of most of us who have from time to time drawn comfort and community from others. But his dramatic isolation was also the wellspring from which he generated his voluminous efforts to connect with the cosmos once again. Though his theme was most often exile and loneliness, his creative output connected him with many readers through the years. While it is true that we can't go home again, it is also true that in a universe of exiles, when people's paths intersect, the journey itself may seem like a home, with the Other present for the while. No small thing.

---

[49] *The Hills Beyond,* pp. 186f.

Clark Moustakis observes:

> Loneliness is a condition of human life, an experience of being human which enables the individual to sustain, extend, and deepen his humanity. . . . Efforts to overcome or escape the existential experience of loneliness can result only in self-alienation. When man is removed from a fundamental truth of life, when he successfully evades and denies the terrible loneliness of individual existence, he shuts himself off from the one significant avenue of his own self-growth.[50]

Moustakis's final point is critical here, for it is precisely when we are thrown back on our own resources that we are obliged to find who we are, of what we are made, and generate from that soul-stuff the richest possible person we can manage in the transient moments we are allowed. It is precisely our aloneness that permits our uniqueness to unfold.

The more we are enmeshed with others, the less differentiated, the less individuated we are; the less individuated, the less we serve the greater purposes of the cosmos for which we were so mysteriously generated. Jung's concept of individuation, far from being an exercise in narcissism, is in fact a humble acquiescence to the great powers that move the stars and stir our sinews. Individuation, by definition, is the advancement of the cosmos through the fullest possible development of the individual who carries that cosmos in a differentiated way. To regress, to seek togetherness, to abstain from the journey toward one's fuller self, is not only soul-crime, it is a denial of the universe itself.

The object relations school of depth psychology asserts that the infant child's experience of the "primal objects," namely the parents, creates a profound phenomenological identification of self and Other, from whose influence we never fully escape. The experience of such attachments, be it smothering or abandoning or some range in between, constitutes a recurrent message about relationship. And the message of the literal dependence of that terribly vulnerable child on its relationships is profoundly overlearned, overconditioned. Thus it becomes difficult later to affirm one's aloneness as a value rather than as a threat of annihilation. Sometimes the apprehension of the possibility of loneliness is rigorously defended against through a projective anger. As Moustakis notes, "Aggres-

---

[50] *Loneliness,* p. ix.

siveness often is a disguise of loneliness anxiety and may be expressed as cynicism and contempt for love and cultural interests."[51]

Perhaps the ideal parent, then, is one who can offer the child support and protection, but also sincere and recurrent affirmation of the child's own inner resources. Then, at the various stages of separation, the child can feel the support those resources offer from within. Nature has not brought us here unequipped for the journey. Rilke wrote to a youth who was anxious and insecure:

> We are set down in life as in the element to which we best correspond. . . .
> We have no reason to distrust our world, for it is not against us. Has it terrors, they are *our* terrors; has it abysses, those abysses belong to us; are dangers at hand, we must try to love them. And if only we arrange our life according to that principle which counsels us that we must always hold to the difficult, then that which now still seems to us the most alien will become what we must trust and find most faithful.[52]

Given the exigencies of childhood vulnerability, and the limits of our power to shape our environment, we inevitably overrate the value of relationship and underrate the value of solitude. (Chekhov wryly observed, "If you are afraid of loneliness, don't get married.")[53] When we are not alone when we are on our own, then we have achieved solitude. The person who attains solitude is alone in his or her unique experience of the journey, yet such a person is conscious of an inner presence with which to dialogue. Out of such dialogue the individuation process moves forward. How tragic, then, the repudiation of such an opportunity for growth. One may only become an individual by giving assent to this dialogue, by conscious and constant valuing of the autonomy and teleology of one's soul.

History is replete with intimations of the value of loneliness. One of the two great unifying mythic patterns (the other being the Eternal Return, the death-rebirth cycle), is the mythologem of the hero quest. Such a quest is the cultural paradigm for the growth of the society. The triune dynamic of the quest is characterized by a) leaving home, which means

---

[51] Ibid., p. 31.
[52] *Letters to a Young Poet,* p. 69.
[53] *Oxford Dictionary of Quotations,* p. 145.

departing the old ego concept, b) enduring the enlargement of consciousness through suffering, and c) achieving a new place, a new home from which one must also, in time, depart. This mythic paradigm is not only a model for individual growth, it is also how a culture's vision is enlarged. In the medieval Grail legend, for example, one is reminded that each of us is obliged to enter the forest where there is no path, for it is shameful to take the path someone has trod before. But what courage, resourcefulness and risk taking one's path demands.

Norma is a thirty-nine-year-old school teacher. She was briefly married to an immature man when she was in her early twenties. Long since divorced, she has grieved her loneliness as a deep, daily anguish even though she has had dozens of brief affairs and one relationship, with another immature man, for a matter of months. Norma alternately hates men, hates herself, is passionately in love, or considers suicide and makes superficial incisions in her wrists because she is not in love. Her life seems to her an iron wheel on which she is bound by an evil fate, doomed to a dreary round of loneliness.

One day she showed up late for her appointment. Fresh, rosy-cheeked, vibrant, it seemed as if the iron wheel that bound her had relented. She eagerly reported that she had spent the day "screwing my brains out" with one of the men most unavailable, most impossible for her. That she would end the evening, or begin the morrow, feeling emptier than before had not yet occurred to her. Norma's love life—strike that, sex life—was compulsive and addictive. As we know, all addictions are anxiety management techniques whether one is conscious of being anxious or not. Whether one reaches out for a cigarette, a drink, a white powder, food or another person, the connection momentarily heals the primal wound we all bear. Loneliness is briefly replaced by fusion with an Other. For that instant one is back in the womb, connected umbilically to the cosmos, but only for the instant, and then, as Rilke had it, loneliness returns and flows onward like the river.

Norma was the child of a narcissistically wounded mother, a woman who slapped her and told her she was an impediment in her mother's life. Her passive father spent his life trying to make enough money to buy objects to fill the emptiness of his life. Norma had known only one connecting, nurturing relationship, that with her nanny whose death when Norma was in college was devastating to her. She frequently visited her nanny's grave and this lost caretaker often showed up in her dreams, especially when she felt most bereft and abandoned.

The consequence most terrible to us all from the primal wounding is not the wound itself, but the distortion it causes in one's sense of self, and the unconscious compulsion to replay analogs of that relationship over and over later in our lives. Norma's experience of her parents, a mother so narcissistic as to be an emotional black hole who sucked in energy and returned no light, and a father so weak as to neither nurture the child nor shield her from his wife's toxic effect, modeled loneliness for her. And so, in all her affairs, she recreated that loneliness.

These distorting relationships cast the mold for Norma. With a grim, inner, unconscious determinism, her wounds influenced her choices as an adult. The loneliness that the adult may just manage to bear is devastating to the child. Norma suffered a dual wounding. On the one hand, the lack of affirmation and support for her as a child was phenomenologically internalized as an objective statement of her lack of worth. This diminished sense of value caused her to choose either men who could not support her, because married or too wounded themselves, or men too weak, like her father, to stand up to her need for constant reassurance.

On the other hand, her emotional abandonment as a child led her to experience the overwhelming terror of loneliness when she was not in a relationship. During these periods she either languished in binging, gorging and purging food, used amphetamines, or, like the day she came late to her appointment, indulged in manic sexual escapades. Such was her addiction in response to the terror of loneliness, a terror she had known throughout her childhood even when her parents were only a room away.

For Norma, the experience of separation exceeded even that of the birth trauma, even the thousand woundings of ordinary life common to us all. Her experience of loneliness neither sustained the growth of a healthy ego nor permitted her to suffer the normal vicissitudes and ambiguities of being in and out of relationships. Her therapy consisted in offering her something of a nurturant, protective environment, and building ego awareness of the nature of projection, transference and repetition compulsion. But beneath the surface there lurked always the great abyss of loneliness.

As we saw above, many character disorders derive from massive wounding in childhood that devastates the ego and renders the person incapable of warm, risking, sharing relationships. Such persons may marry or have multiple relationships, but something is shut down deep within so that either the relationship is sabotaged or no real connection is possible. With such wounding, healing, if at all possible, takes many years of relearning the possibilities inherent in encounters with others.

When Freud was asked what heals in therapy he replied, interestingly enough, that it was love. The love Freud spoke of demands the constant context of care that every child deserves and so few receive, held as they are by parents who themselves are wounded and terrified. Again, just as the acceptance of loneliness is the prerequisite for personal growth and creativity, so the emotional accommodation with loneliness must precede any amelioration of the wounds of the parent-child relationship.

We are asked to bear what is often felt to be unbearable. This is the task awaiting us in the swampland of the soul we call loneliness—to bear the unbearable. But in so doing, by "going through," one breaks the hold of the primal fear that holds sway over much of our lives. To go through it with the insight and courage of an adult, to make friends with it, somehow, breaks that tyrannous hold. The person who cannot bear the emotions attached to the primal wounds cannot escape being a victim.

Norma's story is common, though her suffering no less profound for that. She wonders why she has never had a good relationship, without divining that she herself chooses wrongly, sabotages every relationship by inordinate expectations and demands that drive the other away, resulting in the very loneliness she fears. To realize that in her contemporary relationships she is repeating, analogously, her childhood experience of her parents requires not only courage but an extraordinary act of imagination. In the end, no amount of therapy can help her avoid the loneliness she fears and flees. Some well-meaning friend or counselor might encourage her to find a "better" relationship, but it will be no different as long as she is the same. The only antidote to fear is to go through it. Only by embracing loneliness may its tyranny be broken.

In an interview in *Parabola,* Satish Kumar observed how he learned to walk alone through the world and thereby achieved peace, many friends and his own journey:

> When you accept the state of being a stranger, you are no longer a stranger. . . . I talk about being an exile when everything seemed to be strange around me and everybody was a stranger. Once I had accepted that I didn't have to be part of the world, then I was free to be part of it. This is a paradoxical release of the spirit. This world became mine when I was no longer holding on to it.[54]

The antidote to the fear of losing the world is to let go of it. The antidote for loneliness is to embrace loneliness. As in homeopathy, the wound is healed by swallowing a bit of the toxin itself.

The paradox of relationship, which we in the Western world seem to hold as the cure for all ills, is that the more one can embrace one's separateness, the more one can live with oneself, the better relationship will be. Relationships fail not only because of the personal complexes we all bring to them, but because we ask of them the impossible. Too often, behind the exchange of marriage vows lies the unconscious fantasy that the Other will solve the problem of loneliness.

Most relationships succeed for a while in some sort of fusion, thereby limiting the growth of both parties, or falter under the weight of unreasonable expectations. A healthy relationship is only possible if one is able to come to the table as an individuating isolate. Rilke defined the core of genuine relationship as the sharing of one's solitude with another:

> I hold this to be the highest task of a bond between two people: that each should stand guard over the solitude of the other.[55]

This is the richest offering we can give another, even as we recognize that the other is also alone.

Beyond the terror, the silence of these infinite spaces, lies the richness of one's individual journey. When I try to avoid my journey by transferring it to another, when I capitulate to the fear of loneliness, then I not only violate the unique meaning of my life which it is my summons to

---

[54] "Longing for Loneliness," p. 8.

[55] Cited in John Mood, *Rilke On Love and Other Difficulties,* p. 27.

achieve, I also burden the one I profess to love. And I also thereby sub-
tract my potential part of the richness of the cosmos, the richness which
life is asking me to incarnate. Only in the radical experience of myself as
other—other than my parents, other than you, other than even the one I
was—am I able to experience the often terrifying but always enriching
abundance of life.

In the swampland of doubt and loneliness the task remains: to find the
healthy doubting which pries even Ixion from the iron wheel of the past,
and to live out the loneliness that serves both the achievement of person-
hood and the quality of any relationship. Jung has articulated this mysterious balance:

> Loneliness is not necessarily inimical to companionship, for no one is
> more sensitive to companionship than the lonely man, and companionship
> thrives only when each individual remembers his individuality and does
> not identify himself with others.[56]

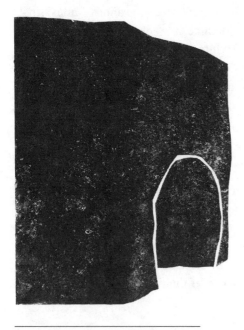

---

[56] *Memories, Dreams, Reflections,* p. 356.

4
Depression, Desuetude and Despair

The Three Corbies

There is an old Scottish ballad called "The Three Corbies," the three ravens. They are hungry and know that soon they will find a recently fallen knight on whom to sup. His hound is already off chasing hares, his hawk seeking a prey, and his lady-love has taken another mate. So they will have the fair knight's bones to house them, his hair to nest them, his flesh to feed them.

So often, it seems, the dread triplets of depression, desuetude and despair sit on the tree outside our window, and, like the three corbies, wait for us to falter and become theirs. Was it not this same dark bird of the soul that haunted Poe in "The Raven"? Did not Winston Churchill call his depression a black beast? Did not the bleak-minded Kafka pun on his own name in describing his depression as a "secret raven"?[57] Have we not all shuddered as these three lurked outside, not only in our dark days of desolation but sometimes even in the splendor of our finest hours?

These three, these corbies, are familiar presences, cawing when we would sleep, flapping across our line of vision, reminding us of the hole in the ground that awaits our end.

Just as the biorhythms of diurnal life, the flux and reflux of hormonal shifts, and even that huge regression of energy we call sleep are normal, so, too, may we expect periodic fluctuations of mood. Could we even imagine the possibility of joy if we could not contrast it with its opposite? Yet, in modern culture we have distorted reality in an addictive search for unalloyed happiness. Such a search can become demonic.

When anything, even a good thing, becomes one-sided and excludes its opposite, the demonic enters in. Even goodness can be demonic when

---

[57] "I don't believe people exist whose inner plight resembles mine; still, it is possible for me to imagine such people—but that the secret raven [kavka in Czech] forever flaps about their heads as it does about mine, even to imagine that is impossible." (The Diaries of Franz Kafka, 1914-1923, p. 195)

we are possessed by it. One thinks of Jung's concept of the shadow as the necessary dark side to every light; indeed, Jung noted, "more light means more night."[58] One thinks of the moral fervor of Puritanism which sacks other churches, the Red Guard with its little red book in hand brutalizing intellectuals, or even, in Philadelphia, the old saying that Quakers came here to do good, and did very well indeed.

Such shadow encounters bring richness to a reality which otherwise would remain superficial, and therein is an invitation to the enlargement of consciousness. Accordingly, we may even say, in a culture which has the infantile fantasy of unmitigated happiness as its goal, depression itself is a manifestation of the shadow.

Perhaps the most functional definition of shadow is *that with which I am uncomfortable in my culture or myself.* Thus the experience of depression may seem like a moral failure, a flaw in the cosmos or an unwelcome visitor to be treated with disdain and diversion. Knowing that fluctuations of mood are normal, inevitable and part of the meaning of our journey, is essential if one is to live without estrangement from self and world.

Depression: The Well with No Bottom

The word "depression" needs clarification. Just as there are *cancers* and *schizophrenias,* so there are *depressions.* Depression may be differentiated as "reactive or environmental," as "endogenous" or "intrapsychic." Frequently they are confused with each other, or one may suffer all three forms at the same time. It is one task of the therapist to help differentiate which depression(s) is or are present.

A reactive depression is a perfectly normal response to a loss or disappointment. One who does not suffer some regression of libido at the failure of a marriage, the death of a friend, or some other significant loss could scarcely be said to have been invested in that outer reality in the first place. A reactive depression is only pathological when it profoundly disrupts one's normal functioning or when the disabling impact of the experience is prolonged beyond a reasonable period.

---

[58] "A Study in the Process of Individuation," *The Archetypes and the Collective Unconscious,* CW 9i, par. 563.

An endogenous depression derives from unknown but presumably biological bases. Typically, such a depression is transmitted genetically and one can usually find other members of one's lineage who have suffered it, though its proper diagnosis was far less precise in earlier generations. Too often such persons berate themselves for the heaviness they carry, have always carried, and consider abnormal. It is as if every day they had to walk uphill to perform the tasks we all perform, though most of us are able to function on a level surface.

One analysand of mine felt that her physical and emotional structure was totally a byproduct of right thinking and right practice. She pursued all sorts of spiritual disciplines in order to get right with God and with the universe, but she remained depressed. Worst of all, she blamed her depression on her own failure to achieve a sufficiently exalted spiritual plateau. When she was treated with one of the new antidepressants her spirits lifted, and she found herself with new energy and optimism. The new serotonin "re-uptake inhibitors" such as Prozac, Paxil, Zoloft and Serzone have substantially improved the quality of life for millions who would otherwise be biologically condemned to an onerous weight on body and soul.

Even after addressing the biological basis of a depression, one may still have the "normal" miseries of life. One of the most difficult cases I ever had to differentiate was that of a twenty-eight-year-old man with cancer. While it was clear enough that the impact of the cancer and its prolonged treatment provided sufficient cause for a reactive depression, he had also had an abusive childhood and would have carried intrapsychic depression in any case. When I learned that he had had depressive patterns even before the cancer, and that there were certain familial biological patterns present, I persuaded him to try an antidepressant. On the twenty-third day of medication he awakened and felt lighter and knew that he was ready for life again, with all its normal miseries.

Depression can feel like a well with no bottom, but from a Jungian perspective intrapsychic depression is a well *with* a bottom, though we may have to dive very deeply to find it. Think of what the word means literally, to de-press, to press down. What is "pressed down"? Life's energy, life's intentionality, life's teleology is pressed down, thwarted, denied, violated. While the etiology of such pressing down may or may not be discernible, something in us colludes with it. We might even say that the quantity and quality of the depression is a function of the quantity and quality of the life force which is being pressed down. Life is warring against life, and we are the unwilling host.

We become the agent of our depressions in various ways. Think of how we unavoidably internalize our circumstances of life, most notably those surrounding our family of origin, in a reflexively reticulated set of assumptions about self, others and relationships. So, for example, a child whose early need for love, security and affirmation is insufficiently met will internalize a false but unavoidable premise. That child will feel unworthy of nurturance since those to whom he or she was given did not, apparently, consider the child worthy; and secondly, as the primary caregivers are the interfacing mediators of the larger world, this early relationship becomes the model for all later ones.

Many of us are burdened with "walking depression," or even "smiling depression." We manage to function well enough, but carry a heavy soul and never feel the lightness which is also part of the journey. Such a depression is common and often undiagnosed. It erodes the quality of one's life. We may collude with it by feeling unworthy and not up to the challenges of life.

The task implicit in this particular swampland is to become conscious enough to discern the difference between what happened to us in the past and who we are in the present. No one can move forward, psychologically, who cannot say, "I am not what happened to me; I am what I choose to become." Such a person can come to recognize that the early deficit was not inherent in the child, but the result of circumstances beyond that child's control. One can then begin to tap the energy for life that was previously walled off.

Jacob was the child of professional parents who held high expectations that he would follow in their path. They were critical of his efforts as a child; if he was not the best at everything he was shamed and degraded. Jacob eventually became a physician, not because of the love of medicine or the healing arts, but because this seemed to be the achievement that would finally gain him his parents' approval and affection. Naturally, the narcissistic needs of the parents remained unexamined and nothing Jacob did was ever quite enough for them. While he was a competent physician and drew some satisfaction from his work, he fell into a profound depression in his late thirties.

Depression at midlife is very common. It seems that there is a necessary and inevitable collision between the false self, reflexively cobbled together as a reaction to the vagaries of childhood, and the natural self which wishes to express itself. This collision of opposites is suffered as a neurosis. Those who choose to remain unconscious of the task their suffering signifies will remain stuck or continue to hurt those around them.

A depression at midlife, or indeed at any time when the psyche wishes enlargement or transition, indicates a suppression of the life force. We become our own worst enemies when we further the split between the natural, instinctual self and the acquired, reactive sense of self. Such a wounding to the impulses of nature will produce a depression whether we make it conscious or not. For this reason, apart from normal fluctuations of mood, everyone experiences depression from time to time. In every case, one has to ask the fundamental question, *what is the meaning of my depression?* The well with no bottom always has a bottom, but we must swim down there to see it. Like Gilgamesh, we are charged with the challenge to find the sacred green watercress of life.

The child, like any plant, will twist and even distort itself in order to gain warmth and light. Jacob distorted himself throughout his life to gain the nurturant energy from his parents, energy which was never forthcoming because their narcissism sucked up energy and gave nothing back. Perhaps Jacob, perhaps we, were meant by nature to be long-distance truck drivers, country-and-western singers, or simply hang out, but we twist and turn in order to find the necessary light. Jacob concluded through his dreams and therapy that he had not been called to become a physician but had done so primarily to gain his parents' approval. That he worked effectively in this elected world was evidence of his ability, but also of a terrible deformation of his soul's intent. Could we not expect depression to follow? Fortunately Jacob possessed the strength of character to dive into his depression, to plummet to the depths of the well. There he began the healing of his soul.

Another man, Edward, inherited his family's business. What many would have seen as walking into a life of power and affluence was experienced by him as a trap. His dreams spoke dramatically of this, but he felt obliged to his spouse, his family, his employees, fated to serve their joint interests. His soul longed to write music and live in a world with other artists, but his duties were clear. When he considered making a move toward his personal dream, he felt overwhelmed by guilt. At this writing Edward remains oppressed by guilt and depression. How long will he be able to sustain the tension between duty and desire? Long enough, we trust, for the transcendent third to appear, at which time he will know his path and his depression will be history.

There is a paradox in the dilemma of Jacob and Edward which touches us all. If Jacob is to become himself, he will have to abandon the legitimate hope of the child for acceptance of himself as he is. Not to let go of this hope, and instead learn to love and affirm himself, means that he will remain depressed. Often, to lift a depression we have to risk taking on that which we fear most, that which is blocking our natural growth. Edward, if he pursues his soul's calling, will likely run directly into that angst which his guilt is a defense against—the anxiety of isolation due to frustrating collective expectations.

Thus we are forced into a difficult choice—anxiety or depression. If we move forward, as our soul insists, we may be flooded by anxiety. If we do not move forward, we will suffer the depression, the pressing down of the soul's purpose. In such a difficult choice one must choose anxiety, for anxiety at least is a path of potential growth; depression is a stagnation and defeat of life.

We may also suffer a generic form of depression. Trapped as so many have been historically, and still are today, in gender limitations, class and economic constraints, depression is a common phenomenon. One may see a depression beneath the surface of an entire country (as I did in Ireland). One may even consider that when one lives in a time whose myths are not consonant with our souls then we may suffer a form of cultural depression as well. If the roles we are asked to serve are not consonant with our inner image, we will often experience the discrepancy as depression without knowing it as such. It is difficult to dive to the bottom of the well when does not even know one is in it.

Jungians see a therapeutic value in neurotic depression. This move of psyche represents a regression of energy in service to the Self, just as our nocturnal regression, sleep, serves the balance and healing of the body and the psyche. If we have left some vital part of ourselves behind, metaphorically speaking, it is essential to go back and down to find it, bring it to the surface, integrate it, live it. Just as the shamans would enter the spirit world to recover that part of the soul which had been split off, and bring it back to reintegrate it, so we are therapeutically obliged to find what has been left behind and bring it back to the surface.

Depth analysts pay close attention to dreams because they come not only from the bottom of the well, but from well below the bottom. So, too, we may encourage the technique of active imagination in order to activate psychic contents that have been repressed. When we are able to render such material conscious, we generally find that the depression lifts. The psyche uses depression to get our attention, to show that something is profoundly wrong. Once we understand its therapeutic value and follow its Ariadne string through our private labyrinth, then depression can even seem a friend of sorts. After all, if we had not hurt so, the psyche would have been already dead. The hurt, the suffering, is a sign that something vital is still there, awaiting our invitation to come back into the world.

In every swampland state, then, is a task. It takes great courage to value depression, to respect it, not to try to medicate it away or distract ourselves from its misery. Down there is potential meaning, split off from consciousness but alive, dynamic. Although a depression robs conscious life of energy, that energy is not gone. It is in the underworld, and like Orpheus who goes down there to confront, perhaps to charm, the lower powers, so we too are obliged to go down into the depression and find our soul's greatest treasure.

Desuetude: The Dispirited Kingdom

What is the difference between spirit and soul? If soul is the purposiveness of life, the investment by nature in the individual, then spirit is the energy, the libido, the eros for the journey. When we are depressed we may say we are dispirited; we have lost the energy for the journey. As we saw above, the energy is still there, but, has sunk to the bottom of the well. Desuetude is the experience of being dispirited, of lacking the energy to traverse the wasteland. Listless, joyless, adrift in anomie—who has not dwelt in such an arid place, periodically, or sometimes for years?

Etymologically, the word "desuetude" means "to grow out of the habit of using." A thousand things may drain off the psychic energy necessary for life: physical illness, the thousand natural shocks which flesh is heir to, fatigue, and of course the effect of complexes that siphon off energy from consciousness. We watch dreams and symptomatology to find where the energy is and where it wants to go, the *Tao* of the moment, so we can track the missing energy.

In the language of the Middle Ages, we all suffer occasionally from *acedia,* spiritual torpor, which was called "the monk's disease." The soul, according to medieval physiology, is moist, and when it is dry one suffers an aridity of the spirit, a wasteland of the psyche. Probably the astringent lifestyle of the monks, the enforced pieties, the vows of poverty, chastity and obedience, not to mention the drab environs, led to a diminishment of the spirit not unlike that which any of us would suffer were we imprisoned. As Max Piper said, "the essence of *acedia* is the refusal to acquiesce in one's own being."[59] To give up one's uniqueness, to sacrifice the personal journey, no matter how normative the superego demands and institutional reinforcements, is to wound the soul. The diminishment of spirits is a concomitant result.

The kindred experience to *acedia* is ennui. Whenever the psyche is channeled, over the long haul, against its autonomous desire, or is obliged to service some value alien to it, ennui will result. Much of modern work is repetitious and constrained within artificial environs. Even professionals are strained through the narrow screens of occupational training, which often cares little for the worth and variety of individual souls. In fact, one could say that the more successful one's outer life, the more rewarded by society, the more likely one may be trapped by that success, a prisoner of constantly escalating obligations and expec-

---

[59] *The Oxford Dictionary of Quotations,* p. 374.

tations. Such success can greatly constrict the soul. Ennui, a most unwelcome visitor, will frequently visit us as we suffer a progressive withdrawal of enthusiasm for our work, a desuetude of desire. Charles Caleb Colton observes, "Ennui has made more gamblers than avarice, more drunkards than thirst, and perhaps as many suicides as despair."[60]

It is in the mythological warp and weft of our age that we are expected to produce more and more, faster and faster, and that we are defined mainly by our observable productivity. Nothing in our time, no sexual scandal, no financial ruin, no lapse in taste, can equal the shaming power of feeling unproductive. We are obliged to repeat ourselves, like successful actors who are typecast, constrained to one role by the public's expectations. More and more, faster and faster, but alas, as Jean Paul Richter noted, "For no one does life drag more disagreeably than for those who try to speed it up."[61]

For our distant ancestors time was a vast colonnade of moments whose corners one could explore at leisure. For us, time is insufficient to the many demands on us. From the freneticism of success, from the obsessive compulsivity of expectations, we suffer ennui and that enervation of the soul we call desuetude.

As with the other swampland states, a psychological task emerges. Life provides us with energy sufficient to the journey. Admittedly, much of it is drained off into pursuits necessary to survival, but when we suffer desuetude we must acknowledge that we have been running against our own grain. Life may be simpler than we in the industrialized nations suppose. Two autonomous acts of psyche are available to us, the feeling function and the flow of energy. These twin resources are infallible guides as to how to live our lives. Any child, any peasant, knows this, of course, but most of us have forgotten.

The feeling function tells us whether something is right for us or not. Unfortunately, many of us have long ago lost contact with this resource and even deliberately override its directives in order to be productive. We do not choose feelings; feelings are autonomous, qualitative analyses of our life. We can only choose to make those feelings conscious, and

---

[60] Ibid., p. 106.
[61] Ibid., p. 867.

then decide whether or not to act on them. Similarly, the ebb and flow of energy, which is a natural function of our mortal state, nonetheless is a vital guide to whether the choices we are making are right for us. If what we are doing is right, the energy is available. Too often we are obliged to channel our feelings and our energy into a soulless task. We learn to do this because we are rewarded for it and would feel shame if we stopped.

Yet in the experience of desuetude, in the collusion with soullessness, the task of consciousness vibrates. Jung's question haunts us all—what task is this person avoiding? In most cases, we are avoiding responsibility for our lives. In childhood we learn, overlearn, our powerlessness; we internalize authority figures and societal norms and later, as adult worker ants, serve them slavishly. To run counter to them causes us inauthentic guilt and anxiety. But the experience of desuetude, getting out of the habit of using our energy to serve the soul, leads us further and further away from our authentic selves.

Only by faithfully observing our loss of energy can we track it to its split-off place. Lost energy is retrievable. If we choose to serve the soul, the energy comes back and then serves us. The responsibility of choosing to live the life we are called to, with all its practical exigencies and commitments to others, remains ours. Desuetude is a protest of the soul which autonomously removes energy from us because it does not approve of how ego is investing it. Such a powerful statement from the unconscious may be ignored, but then we may expect our symptoms to intensify. The soul will not be mocked. Its rumblings, however unwelcome, are really friendly warnings to change our lives. When we attend to that task, the energy returns.

Despair: The Darkest Corby

Despair is to be without hope, without prospects, without alternatives. In the Judeo-Christian tradition, despair is a sin for it infringes on God's autonomy, limits the Limitless, constricts the Creator. In many ways, despair may be seen as the worst of the dismal states for it seems to offer no way out. Despair closes off even the heroic defiance of Shelley, who in *Prometheus Unbound*[62] commands that we "hope till hope creates

---

[62] *Prometheus Unbound,* in *The Poems of Shelley,* p. 268.

from its own wreck the thing it contemplates." Similarly, the English Prime Minister Benjamin Disraeli, who certainly knew defeat, prejudice and loss, argued that "despair is the conclusion of fools."[63]

But who among us has not known despair, when the forces aligned against us, outer or inner, seem so much greater than our petty powers to defeat, even resist? Who has not wished for the surcease of defeat, even death, to end the terrible tension, the agony of ambiguity? Who has not fled, lemming-like, into the jaws of despair, preferring the horror known over the horror imagined? Camus argued in *The Myth of Sisyphus* that suicide is the only truly philosophical problem; to be or to be—that is the question. If we embrace despair and commit suicide, even then we have chosen. But we have chosen a path which admits no vital outcome. Staying alive, embracing the despair and the awful pull of opposites at least keeps open the possibility of resolution, of some forward movement.

James Hillman, in *Suicide and the Soul,* argues that even in the moment of despair, when one wishes to die, one does not really wish to die. One wishes, rather, instantaneous transformation. The counsel this blackest of corbies whispers in our ear is that this decisive act will bring resolution, when all it brings is cessation. If one can embrace the implicit wish for transformation, says Hillman, one may catalyze the dynamic of change. Otherwise, one is not around to profit from any benefits thought to accrue from the decisive act.

Yet talk is cheap, and within the rhetorical circle which despair represents, any argument is quickly refuted by hopelessness. Any alternative becomes a straw man easily tumbled by the logic of the irresolvable. Despair is tautological; it begs the question; it argues in a circle, and seldom is there a point of egress from this cycle of hopelessness.

I can think of no rumination on despair that equals the 1885 poem by Gerard Manley Hopkins, "Carrion Comfort." Hopkins was a Jesuit whose private agonies existed side by side with his daily priestly ministrations. He wrote because he had to, because he needed the confessional for himself, because he needed some space in which to work with his soul's swampland. His aesthetic sensibility, his manipulation of language

---

[63] *Oxford Dictionary of Quotations,* p. 185.

and concept, and his unique style have marked him as one of the true progenitors of modernist literature, but in his lifetime only a very few ever saw his poems or sensed his struggle. Many of his poems, "Carrion Comfort" among them, are now called "the terrible sonnets," for they depict the terrors of a soul in peril.

> Not, I'll not, carrion comfort, Despair, not feast on thee;
> Not untwist—slack they may be—these last strands of man
> In me or, most weary, cry *I can no more.* I can;
> Can something, hope, wish day come, not choose not to be.
> But ah, but O thou terrible, why wouldst thou rude on me
> Thy wring-world right foot rock? lay a lionlimb against me? scan
> With darksome devouring eyes my bruised bones? and fan,
> O in turns of tempest, me heaped there; me frantic to avoid thee and flee?
>
> Why? That my chaff might fly; my grain lie, sheer and clear.
> Nay in all that toil, that coil, since (seems) I kissed the rod,
> Hand rather, my heart lo! lapped strength, stole joy, would laugh, cheer.
> Cheer whom though? the hero whose heaven-handling flung me, foot trod
> Me? or me that fought him? O which one? is it each one?
>   That night, that year
> Of now done darkness I wretch lay wrestling with (my God!) my God.[64]

In the force and fever of Hopkins's sprung rhythm, one senses the power of his struggle and its sincerity, and that one cannot afford too many victories like this one.

Notice how the circuitous logic of despair casts even expository statements as negatives, " Not, I'll not . . . not . . . . Not . . ." One feels that he has been all but completely unstrung in his faith, all but dehumanized, and yet he finds the strength for one final battle. We see that what he struggles against is more than awesome. The Being who contests his soul is phenomenologically named "O thou terrible," and has the world-wringing power to rock him, to weigh on him, to scan him right to the bottom of his soul. Who could survive such an encounter? Who would not flee into the sweetmeat of despair, not feast on such carrion, the dead matter of soul's defeat?

Hopkins feels that his despair has grown even since he kissed the staff

---

[64] *Norton Anthology of Poetry*, p. 858.

of the cross in his vows of obedience. And yet something in him intuits that his soul is working its way out, suffering its way through on some great plain, some soul-sized prospect. Hopkins intuits that he is cast as Divine Antagonist against the Divine Protagonist. His *agon,* his struggle, is on a supraordinary plain. He fights with God, the heaven-handling hero, and yet he, too, in suffering the *agon* of despair rather than giving into it, seems, like Job, blessed in the terrible encounter with the Divine. It is "my God!"—his God who so blesses him as to blast him with the terrible largeness of the journey.

There is no "cheap grace" here, to use Dietrich Bonhoeffer's phrase.[65] If one survives, one is blessed, but who would rush to take the ride? As Hopkins reminds us in another "terrible sonnet,"

> O the mind, mind has mountains; cliffs of fall
> Frightful, sheer, no-man-fathomed. Hold them cheap
> May who ne'er hung there.[66]

Out of the soul's tumult, out of genuine despair, Hopkins wrings meaning. He learned, and came to affirm, the terrible election of encountering the depths of being. In his *agon,* as perilously close as he comes to annihilation, we discern that he retains a measure of dignity that saves him. It is the quality of his struggle, quite apart from the outcome, which brings him triumph. We think of the heroic despair of the Celtic Cuchulain who wades out to sea, slashing with his sword in the despairing hope beyond hope. We sense in their desire to fall on the field of despairing combat that the heroes merit their Valhalla after all. The heart, if not the mind, agrees with Tennyson's aged wanderer:

> Death closes all, yet some work of noble note
> may yet be done, not unbecoming those
> who strove with gods.[67]

In this heroic impulse one moves out of victimage. Apart from outcomes, apart from resolution or victory, one senses the redeeming worth of the struggle itself. The Prometheus of Aeschylus and Shelley, bound

---

[65] *Letters and Papers from Prison,* p. 112.
[66] "No Worst, There is None," in *Norton Anthology of Poetry,* p. 858.
[67] "Ulysses," in ibid., p. 704.

by a vengeful Zeus, is nonetheless free, and almighty Zeus trembles before that great freedom. Camus' Sisyphus, bound by the gods to push the boulder up the hill endlessly, only to watch it fall, endlessly, is yet freer than the gods who oppress him. By choosing to push, rather than be doomed to push, Sisyphus wrests that saturnian power away from the gods and retains his dignity. In such movements of soul one attains the *tragic* sensibility. The opposite of the tragic sense of life is *pathos,* from which we get "pathetic." Tragedy, with its inevitable defeat, is an active, heroic embrace of life's *agon.* Passive suffering is victimage, pathetic.

The task implicit in the encounter with despair is to sustain the struggle, to move from being victim to being hero, from the pathetic to the tragic. The human condition, of course, ends in death, which may be seen as a defeat, or it may be seen as the wisdom of nature, or the gods, which transcends the petty powers of ego to comprehend. But the task implicit in despair is not to deny the terrible feelings, nor to relinquish the modest dignity of our humanity, but to suffer through toward whatever awaits beyond the tautologies of despair.

These terrible corbies—depression, desuetude and despair—will always nest just outside the window. No matter how conscientiously we strive to be quit of them, they will return, again and again, their cacophonous cries interrupting the sleep of denial. Let us think of them as constant reminders of our task. Even in their cawing, noisome presence we have choices to make.

5
Obsessions and Addictions

A Season in Hell

Did we ever stop to reflect on what makes Hell hellish, or how and why the idea of Hell even emerged? What was Dante's *catabasis* all about, or *Paradise Lost,* or Rimbaud's *Une Saison d'Enfer?* By the time we reach midlife, if we are introspective at all, the thought has occurred that the only constant in our lives has been ourselves. However much we might wish to blame our parents, society or our partners for our problems, we are stuck with the recurrent encounter with ourselves.

My midlife experience at the Jung Institute in Zürich was typical. Naturally I assumed it would be like other graduate school programs and I knew how to navigate them. Instead, the experience was more like that of a Zen *koan.* I was the question, I the problem; what I had become was now the obstacle. The not-I was perhaps the only answer. Naturally the ego would wish to cling to its position, fortify its assumptions, but it was the ego that had to be dismantled. As the popular saying has it, everywhere I go, there I am. Or as Milton observed,

> Me miserable! which way shall I fly
> Infinite wrath, and infinite despair?
> Which way I fly is Hell; myself am Hell.[68]

Or recall Christopher Marlowe's Dr. Faustus: "Why this is hell, nor am I out of it."[69] And:

> Hell hath no limits nor is circumscrib'd
> In one self place, where we are is hell,
> And where Hell is, there must we ever be.[70]

What is most hellish about Hell is that it is endless. We can bear anything if it has an end. What is hellish is to be without hope, without

---

[68] *Paradise Lost,* lines 73-75.
[69] *The Tragical History of Dr. Faustus,* line 76.
[70] Ibid., lines 120-122.

surcease, without relief. To be stuck is hellish. Looking at Dante's vision of Hell as concentric circles of deepening moral turpitude, one sees that his vision of moral consequence is that one is stuck in the symbolic extension of what one has chosen.

The flatterers, for example, having spread the stuff in their lives, are immersed in excrement to their lower lip. As they are obliged to continue being themselves forever, so their mouths will be filled with liquid shit. The materialists? They are doomed to an eternity of rolling large boulders back and forth. The gluttonous are doomed because they misunderstood what really fed, misunderstood what true soul food was. At the centermost circle of Hell, the betrayers are immersed in ice; their coldness of heart is now their eternal punishment.

Dante's vision, then, is that we become what we were, but more so, and moreover we are stuck with it. This begins to sound familiar, for who is not becoming more and more what one already is, feeling doomed to the repetition compulsion? Why this is Hell, then, and we are it.

Obsessions: Ideas Unbidden

An obsession is an idea that invades consciousness with sufficient power to supplant the will. This usurpation of consciousness naturally causes us anxiety, quickly followed by reflexive behavior whose purpose is to assuage the urgency of the unbidden idea. We all have obsessive thoughts and we all have compulsions which follow.

Sometimes our obsessive-compulsive dramas are conscious, sometimes not. At times we evolve personal rituals based on magical thinking, whose purpose is to lower our level of anxiety; we indulge in behaviors such as blinking, twisting our fingers and so on, without even realizing what we are doing. Normally these behaviors remain low-grade interruptions of consciousness and we tolerate them. Sometimes they take over and seriously interfere in our lives.

Roger was a thirty-five-year-old man who sold commercials for radio stations. He was happily married with two daughters. His work required him to be on the road every day. Whenever he saw an attractive woman, had a thought about one, or even heard certain songs, he was compelled to find a pay phone and call his wife to tell her of his quite ordinary thoughts. At first his wife was amused; then she began to wonder if there was fire under that smoke, and finally she became irritated by the constant interruptions. She insisted he seek therapy to get rid of his problem.

The more pervasive the unbidden idea, the more primal its origins and the more intractable it will prove. Roger had been raised by a devout, puritanical mother who took full control of his childhood. His father was long deceased. Any thoughts of the body, of sexuality, even of a woman, were contaminated for Roger by the direct indoctrination of his overwhelming mother. This deep split between his nature and his acculturation was furthered by his parochial education and the overlay of guilt about anything sexual. Many years later, Roger suffered the activation of this split whenever he observed a woman attractive to him or had a sexual fantasy.

As we saw earlier, most often guilt is a defense against anxiety. Thus Roger was ridden by guilt over the most natural of thoughts, and his immediate compulsion was to lower this distress by confessing to his wife as if she were a stern nun or a suspicious mother. It was quite difficult for Roger even to acknowledge that he was reenacting his childhood fears and making his wife into his mother. So deep was the split that the obsessive ideas and the concomitant guilt persisted. While he could not, through force of consciousness alone, root out the old idea, he did manage to change his behavior and write down his confessions for his analyst rather than pester his wife.

In George, too, the wound was deep. He recalled the day at age nine when he saw his mother walk out the door, get in a stranger's car, look back at him without expression and ride away forever. When he was married years later he was convinced his wife would also leave him. He followed her, sought to control her life, fantasized about her being with another man. On their anniversary they went on a trip to a distant city. While he was in the shower, room service arrived. In that brief moment, George convinced himself that his wife had had a liaison with her mystery lover. When she suggested he get therapy, he insisted that she be hypnotized to tell the truth and also take multiple polygraphs—which she did and passed.

Like Roger, George had suffered a primal wounding and made his wife his mother even as Oedipus had made his mother his wife. Sadly, for both, the wounding was so primal as to be unreachable and undissolvable. Cognitive therapy, behavioral modification, active imagination—nothing could shake their obsessive delusions.

There are examples where the obsession, hurtful as it may be, can actually fuel creativity or provide a raison d'être for one's life. When the sculptor Henry Moore was asked how he remained so creative over so many decades, he replied that he had a passion so great that he had not been able to chisel it all away.

The Nobel Prize-winning poet William Butler Yeats similarly suffered a fifty-year obsession. In 1889 he met the beautiful Irish revolutionary Maud Gonne, standing in the doorway framed with apple blossoms. Then began, he later said, the great misery of his life. Fifty years later, while on his death bed he still wrote of her. He followed her everywhere. He proposed marriage repeatedly and was rebuffed. He offered to give up writing and devote himself to her world, but she continued on her political ways toward "The Troubles" which constitute the tragic history of Ireland. She was, he knew, on a doom-bound journey from which he could not save her. He wrote about her instead.

> A girl arose that had red mournful lips
> And seemed the greatness of the world in tears,
> Doomed like Odysseus and the laboring ships
> And proud as Priam murdered with his peers.[71]

Through the decades his magnificent obsession with Maud Gonne persisted. At times he even felt suicidal, despairing, pathetic.

> But I, being poor, have only my dreams;
> I have spread my dreams under your feet;
> Tread softly because you tread on my dreams.[72]

When Maud married a soldier of fortune, John McBride, Yeats felt doubly rejected; not only had she chosen someone else, she had chosen his opposite. Later, when McBride was executed by the British after the

---

[71] "The Sorrow of Love," in *Selected Poems and Two Plays of William Butler Yeats,* p. 14.
[72] "He Wishes for the Cloths of Heaven," in ibid., p. 27.

abortive Easter Rising of 1916, Yeats rushed over and renewed his proposal. Maud refused again. Driven mad for the moment by his obsession, Yeats proposed marriage to her young daughter Iseult, who wisely knew a bad idea when she saw it. On the rebound he married an English woman and had a happy and productive marriage with two children, but his thoughts remained with Maud even as he lay dying.

Students of literature may be grateful for Maud's tough line with Yeats for, in Auden's phrase about Ireland, she "hurt him" into poetry. Yeats admits how willing he would have been to sacrifice his talent for her hand:

> That had she done so who can say
> What would have shaken from the sieve?
> I might have thrown poor words away
> And been content to live.[73]

Yeats's magnificent obsession fueled his poetry. Unlike the obsessions of Roger and George, he was at least able to sublimate his suffering into art. There is no accounting for why this particular woman so activated his unconscious anima-image that she grew to such proportions in his psychic economy.

In the phenomenon of stalking, one sees another result due to the projection of some vital element of one's psyche onto another person. Such obsessional thinking must not be confused with love; it is pure projection and in most cases will reflect some aspect of the original parent-child dyad. Just as the parent holds sway over the psyche of the dependent child, so the wounds, the fused identities, the deepest dynamics of relationship, become hard-wired into the psychic main frame. What is unconscious remains repressed until activated, at which time it is projected onto another. An obsessional projective identification occurs when the other is charged with carrying our missing piece, thus becoming the carrier of our well-being, or alternatively our greatest threat.

Falling in love happens through projective identification. What feels so good about the "in love" state is that the other is, for the moment, able to reflect our missing piece(s) back to us. The sense of euphoria arises

---

[73] "Words," in ibid., p. 32.

from the momentary intimation of our own wholeness. Obviously the other also has qualities different from those in our own unconscious. Accordingly, the projection may not last for long; when reality replaces fantasy, indifference, even hatred at the revealed "inadequacies" of the other, often replaces "love." We all know how obsessional love can be because it carries our primal projects, not only those left over from childhood but also those derived from the existential dilemma, of being alone on a spinning planet hurtling through a great emptiness.

Just as Roger and George are trapped in the child's need for a parent, so Yeats was trapped in his projection onto a woman who was, as much evidence suggests, wholly unsuitable as a partner to him. What could not be owned, made conscious, thus became an obsession. The unbidden idea carries a large amount of affect which threatens the homeostasis of the psyche. Thrown off balance, we act out in ways that may seem irrational and destructive but are logical consequences of the unconscious idea.

Clearly the task confronting us in this dismal place is to make the unconscious dynamic conscious. As this is a most difficult task, sometimes impossible because unbearable, our obsessions persist and we remain in Hell. As we have noted, because the unbidden idea is usually rooted in primal experience, often from childhood, we are summoned to confront the very thing that was too large for the child to bear or assimilate. It is the reflexive memory of that unbearable quantity of affect that keeps an obsession functioning.

The adult is capable of bearing the unbearable. To wit: "I am alone, really alone. No one is really there for me." "I can be hurt, powerfully hurt." "They will not take care of me, or meet my needs." "I am afraid of pain, and afraid of being afraid." "I do not have the resources to carry the burden of my own journey. I will perish if the other does not rescue me."

There, it is said. These are the sorts of secrets buried so deeply, working their ineluctable way through our souls, that we can neither face them nor outgrow them. But they will not go away, and they enter unbidden when we most seek control over our lives. They remind us of our fragility; they make us feel like failures; they shame and degrade us. And yet the task remains to face them, the unbearable thoughts, so they finally lose their tyrannous power. Jung noted, "Most of my patients knew the deeper truth, but did not live it."[74] Which is to say, unless we live our deeper truths, we will spend many more seasons in Hell.

Addictions: Astride Ixion's Wheel

Ixion, who had the effrontery to attempt the seduction of Hera, was condemned by an indignant Zeus to being bound to a wheel that turned continuously in Hades. (Interestingly, only the beautiful music of Orpheus could stop the wheel, and then only temporarily. Similarly, Yeats's obsession was only assuaged by the beautiful music he sometimes wrung from his soul's distress.)

Ixion's plight is familiar to us all. An obsessional thought followed by a compulsive act ties us to a round of the "same old same old." What smoker does not experience self-loathing upon repeated failed efforts to stop? What drinker does not drink to assuage the guilt of his last drink? What compulsive eater does not shudder at the added adipose? Who does not feel trapped in the iron circle of self-defeating thoughts and behaviors, even those most adept at self-control or social achievement?

Rather than see the alcoholic as a loser, as a person lacking in will, many have seen him or her as most invested in the need for control of the sense of self. Gregory Bateson, for example, has suggested that the compulsive drinker believes he or she can conjure with the spirits and control them.[75] So challenged, the game is on and the spirits usually win. But then the drinker is challenged again to a new test of will, if not a rigid sobriety which sooner of later will succumb to the pressures of everyday life, to the fantasy of control of the uncontrollable. Thus, the emotional pain the drinker seeks to medicate becomes secondary to the test of strength in which he or she is conscripted. The cycle can only escalate until, as Alcoholics Anonymous insists, the person recognizes his or her actual powerlessness in the face of the test.

Jung pointed out to the founders of AA that "the craving for alcohol [is] the equivalent, on a low level, of the spiritual thirst of our being for wholeness," an implicit attempt to connect with a higher power.[76] The

---

[74] "The Aims of Psychotherapy," *The Practice of Psychotherapy*, CW 16, par. 108.
[75] See Gregory Bateson, *Steps to an Ecology of Mind*, p. 86.
[76] See Jan Bauer, *Alcoholism and Women*, appendix 3.

physiology of alcohol, or any mood-altering drug, offers a brief promise of this connectedness and then yanks it away. One must continue in order to anesthetize this new pain, and so it goes.

Only through a surrender of the fantasy of control, suffering thereby not only the loss of ego domination but the pain of the pain, may one experience a release from Ixion's wheel. This is not unlike the experience of surrendering one's will to divine powers—"not my will but Thine."

Jungian Analyst Marion Woodman has written in a very feeling fashion about the hellishness of Ixion's wheel.

> Behind the masks of these successful lives, there lurks disillusionment and terror. One common factor appears repeatedly. Consciously the individuals are being driven to do better and better within the rigid framework they have created for themselves; unconsciously they cannot control their behavior. There are countless individual and collective reasons for the outbreak of chaos as soon as the daily routine is completed. Will power can only last so long. If that will power has been maintained at the cost of everything else in the personality, then nothingness gapes raw. When in the evening it's time to come back to oneself, the mask and the inner Being do not communicate. . . . Compulsions narrow life down until there is no living—existence perhaps, but no living.[77]

Woodman notes that the framework, the wheel of Ixion, is created by ourselves though we do not yet know that. Whatever structure we have erected to bolster our shaky sense of self, our addictive patterns are defenses against angst whether we know it or not. All addictions are in fact anxiety management techniques. When the psychic material to which such affect is attached is activated, our psyche begins its defense.

As the angst mounts, we indulge in some repetitive behavior that allows us to "connect." With that connection the anxiety temporarily recedes. Such behavior can occur entirely without our conscious volition or acknowledgment. A person can light a cigarette, smoke it, extinguish it and continue a conversation without conscious interruption. Unfortunately, the salubrious effects of the momentary connection do not persist and so the behavior must be repeated the next time angst-ridden material is activated. Ixion's wheel turns, bringing one back to where one began.

---

[77] *Addiction to Perfection: The Still Unravished Bride,* p. 12.

As Woodman notes, it is impossible to keep the chaos permanently at bay, impossible not to sense the ground shift ominously beneath our feet, and so the palliative behavior turns the wheel in its closed cycle. Again, guilt, shame, failure follow quickly in the repetitions we hope would free us but only entrap us further. Yet, surely we are not to blame for having been wounded, for being fragile, for feeling fear. The task of this dismal state of addictions, again, is to risk bearing the unbearable. What cannot be borne consciously will be projected onto a person, a substance, a behavior, and the wheel turns anew.

There are no Hells more hellish than addictions, for nothing seems more conclusively our own fault. "Which way I fly is hell; myself am Hell." But what we are enslaved by is an idea, an idea always derivative in character, anchored in the past, primal and unassimilated. We must remember that when such an idea traps us in the past, it also constricts us to the limitations of childhood. Such ideas narrow our lives; they are reductionist in origin and consequence, defenses against the angst which is the necessary concomitant of growth. Roger and George seem doomed to replicate the mother-child relationship, thereby sabotaging the potential enlargement of their adult lives. Yeats at least converted his suffering to the stuff of art and momentarily found relief from Ixion's wheel.

Our task, and terrifying it is, is to burrow into the obsession, deconstruct the addiction, to find the primal, unassimilated idea buried so deeply. Then, as adults, we may be able to bear the unbearable, think the unthinkable, suffer the insufferable, in order to be free.

Ixion's wheel turns silently, inexorably, as I write and you read. None of us can be conscious all the time, and the guilt and shame that attends our many shortcomings erodes precisely the strength necessary to confront the unthinkable. To go down into the anxiety state, to feel what we really feel, is to "go through" and break the tyranny of the timeless emotions that haunt us. We are Hell; unwittingly we have constructed it, and reflexively we serve it. The harrowing of Hell is the only way through to that aperture which Dante espied after his fearful journey. Only the descent into Hades can free us from Hades.

6
Anger

Feeding the Three-Headed Dog

In Greek mythology the Underworld is guarded by a mad, three-headed dog named Cerberus. Dante, and his guide Virgil, evade Cerberus's ravening jaws by jamming earth into his triple maw and then pass by. We are seldom so successful in avoiding his rabid bite.

In the physiology of the Middle Ages, perfect health in humans was thought to be achieved by the balancing of the four elemental fluids, called *humours*. It was also believed that our character and personality traits resulted from a greater or lesser amount of these humors, and a significant imbalance produced a pathologized personality. Ben Jonson, Shakespeare's contemporary, satirized these typologies in his *Every Man in His Humour*.

The fluids, and their pathologized forms, are as follows. Black bile in too great a measure produced melancholia, or depression. It was no accident that Shakespeare attired his melancholy Dane in black, for his audience would automatically associate a psychological state with such an iconographic color. Too much green bile (phlegm) produced a phlegmatic disposition, a lazy or lethargic personality. Too much yellow bile produced a bilious personality, peevish and ill-tempered. And too much red bile (choler) produced the choleric personality, an angry, red-faced disposition—the mad dog, Cerberus.

Why is Cerberus three-headed? One might surmise that there are three kinds of anger, or perhaps three origins of anger. The etymological root of the words *anger, angst, anxiety* and *angina* comes from the Indo-Germanic *angh,* which means "to constrict." When the organism is constricted in its natural spontaneity, it may suffer anger, anxiety or somatic distress. Yet for many, anger was not tolerated in the family circle. Thus, when the child felt the wounding of psychic "constriction," the unacceptable emotional response was channeled into acting out, repression as depression, or widening a shadow split within.

93

It is no accident that sexuality and anger are the most problematic of shadow encounters, for they are experienced by the ego world, and the collective, as anarchic, disruptive to social order, outside of one's control. But as existential "constriction" is unavoidable, so anger is inescapable. All of us have pockets of anger floating about in our psyche, just as we have pockets of sadness and fear. Since many of us were enjoined against the honest expression of emotion, most notably anger and sexuality, we carry these split-off emotions unconsciously. Sometimes they remain repressed as a long-term, low-grade depression; sometimes they lie very close to the surface and erupt with damaging effect to oneself and others. Sometimes one has suffered a wounding of such magnitude as to remain dominated by anger.

A number of years ago an autobiographical book appeared in Switzerland titled *Mars* (the Roman god of war and anger), written by a man whose pseudonym was Fritz Zorn. *(Zorn* is the German word for rage; his real family name was Angst.) In this remarkable, passionate, vitriolic book Zorn lashed out at his family of origin and his Swiss bourgeois culture. Born to wealth and privilege, he had also been a prisoner of the tyranny of expectations, the weight of the Swiss collective psychology which was, and remains, very constricted, very proper, very demanding. Now, in his late twenties, Zorn was dying of cancer. He was not only enraged because he realized that he had not lived his life, he attributed his cancer to the somatization of the constrictive environment at work on him. His unattended, unexpressed anger had become malignant rage. (There is some fragmentary evidence to suggest that those who have special difficulty expressing anger are more prone to have their auto-immune system suppressed and be susceptible to cancer.)

In *Mars* Zorn tears at his socially prominent family with their normative demands, at Swiss culture, and at the fate which had given him this life and was now snatching it away. In writing *Mars,* which became a bestseller in Switzerland, a *success de scandale,* Zorn hoped to purge himself of his malignant rage and save himself from the metastases slowly suffocating him. He raced his cancer to finish the book and free himself. On the day before he died he learned that his book had been accepted by a publisher. The anger which could not be seen, which had gone underground into the cellular level, would now, finally, be expressed. His book became a bestseller because he expressed what so many could not.

In *The Middle Passage* I pointed out how we have all suffered the wounding of too-much-ness, the overwhelming of the child's permeable boundaries by the outer world, or not-enough-ness, the insufficient response, neglect or abandonment of the child's needs by its environment. As a result of these wounds, one misreads the nature of the world, colludes in the deformation of one's own nature, and adopts a set of reflexive responses as a kind of false self whose purpose is to manage the level of anxiety. Accordingly, one who feels overwhelmed by the environment, Daddy's alcoholism, say, or Mommy's depression, tends to acquire a passive, co-dependent personality in order to survive. The child who suffers the insufficiency of its environment tends to develop a diminished sense of self-worth and addictively pursue affirmation and reassurance from others. In both cases, the child unwittingly colludes in self-estrangement. In both cases the person will be carrying a great deal of anger, given the constriction of the natural self, though this anger may be unacknowledged.

Further, there is a third kind of wounding which occasions anger: the conscious or barely conscious intimation that we are somehow willing participants in this self-wounding. We all know, though we may not wish to admit it, that we are our own worst enemies, and that we live, in Sartre's phrase, in *mauvaise foi,* bad faith, with ourselves and others. This third anger is ultimately directed toward ourselves. And Cerberus is a three-headed dog.

Gerald was the child of a father who was twenty years older than the mother. By the time Gerald was a boy and needed his father for mentoring, the father was elderly and ailing. When Gerald reached puberty his father died. As there were no wise elders of the village to help him bridge up and out of the regressive powers of his mother complex, Gerald drifted through life. His mother continued to support him, and was glad to do so, for she had promoted Gerald to be her surrogate companion. Gerald carried his need for the lost father as a deep melancholy, a sadness he could not name but which dominated his psyche. He sought ther-

apy in his late thirties because of the desuetude he felt and only then realized the depth of his fatherless wound.

Gerald hated his mother for he knew she had co-opted his adulthood,
albeit not without his collusion. Because of his deep ambivalence thereby
toward the feminine, Gerald had never committed himself to a relationship. Unconsciously, he transferred to the contemporary woman in his
life the power wielded by the mother in his psyche. Fearing that power,
he stayed on the periphery of relationship and found himself grinding
away with anger toward women. He was never verbally or physically
abusive, but he did vent his rage at those he believed were trying to control him. At the same time, he drifted through life without professional
commitment too. It was a revelation to him that he was also angry at "the
old man," whom he had barely known because his father had been there
neither as mentor nor to provide a masculine balance to the feminine.

In a speech to the Philadelphia Jung Center in April, 1992, Jungian
analyst Guy Corneau of Montreal, author of *Absent Fathers, Lost Sons,*
cited the example of a child who had suddenly turned violent as he entered school. The child had been raised by a caring mother, but there had
been no father. The child did not grasp that there were fathers until he entered school and saw some children picked up at day's end by their fathers. These were the children he attacked. He was filled with anger by
the constriction of his developmental needs, angry at the deficit, that is.

So too Gerald, who knew he hated women because he feared their
power, discovered that he also harbored great anger toward his absent father. This recognition was the turning point in his therapy. Making conscious the wound of not-enough-ness, and his need for mentoring, helped
lift his negative energy off women and channel it in the direction of the
missed mentoring. He then was able to use his therapy as a rite of passage out of the domination of the mother complex, as a mentoring which
partially filled the father void, and as a bridge into his adulthood.

Gerald's anger was in fact a legitimate response to his early wounding, but he had first suffered that anger as desuetude, then transferred it
wrongly to women, then attacked the ghost of his father who haunted
him. Once the reasons for the anger, the healthy motives behind it, could
be identified, his energy was freed to address the proper task of growing

up in a less than perfect world. By the end of his therapy, Gerald was able to form a relationship, marry and find his life's work as well.

Jayne was the sort of person everyone turns to for help. As an adolescent she had thought of being a nurse but became a social worker instead. Both her parents were alcoholics. Even as a child, Jayne had been the designated peace maker, problem solver and mother to her younger siblings. Those other children had grown up to various drug and alcohol difficulties of their own. But Jayne was not one who ever felt she had the luxury of her own feelings. She smiled at everyone, carried their burdens and was widely liked. Jayne's life seemed to work perfectly—she was a productive therapist and knew who she was.

However, Jayne was frequently devastated by migraines. She tried every medication, hypnosis, biofeedback—all of which were marginally helpful. In desperation she entered analysis. Unlike Gerald, who knew he was angry but whose anger was misdirected, Jayne was blissfully unaware of her anger. She saw herself as a cheerful, sunny sort, and so she was, but she was sitting on a mountain of anger, not only for the abusive overwhelment of her childhood, but, at a far deeper level, for its deformation of her soul.

Jayne had always lived in that valley of depression which comes from anger turned inward. She attacked the only person she had permission to attack—herself. Beneath her sunny persona lurked rage. Energy of that quality and magnitude had to go somewhere. The child she once was had no permission to express its genuine needs, its outrage. So she stuffed all that and hid behind a persona that would offend no one, and, in time, so identified with this false, caretaker self that she unconsciously rolled it over into a profession whereby she could continue her treatment of the wounded family of humanity. However efficacious she was in her work, however much lauded for her contributions, she remained the wounded child who could only maintain her fragile estate by an existential lie.

The turning point in Jayne's therapy occurred when her parents, having lived in another part of the country, moved back to her city. The headaches blasted her and she realized that not only would the parents want her to resume her caretaking role, but that she was afraid not to. The fear she felt, initially defended against by her guilt, was the fear of the child who has no outer options and is obliged to adapt to the Realpolitik of the family.

When her guilt, fear and headaches were confronted it became possible for her to see that they were defenses against the mountain of anger on which she sat. When she could speak the unspeakable, when she could express her rage and say No to the parents, her headaches stopped. Confronting her parents was literally the most difficult thing in her life. Despite the child's overwhelming fear within, she was now an adult and could draw boundaries where none had existed before.

The abuse which had attended Jayne's childhood had been internalized and became toxic. Where else could a "nice" girl put her rage except back into herself? Her self-punishing dynamic is reminiscent of William Blake's 1794 poem, "The Poison Tree."

> I was angry with my friend:
> I told my wrath, my wrath did end.
> I was angry with my foe:
> I told it not, my wrath did grow.[78]

Then the speaker in the poem waters this malignant growth with fears, with tears, with smiles and with wiles, exactly as Jayne had learned to do. In time the fruit from that forbidden tree turns toxic and hurts not only others but also the one in whose soul it grows. The poison tree, like the Edenic tree, bears bitter fruit, such as migraines, and can only be uprooted by the cleansing catharsis which the child could not have afforded. Jayne could risk the onslaught of emotions against which she had necessarily defended herself because the migraines were even worse, and because she was finally strong enough to recognize the anger she had always carried. This anger was not only a legitimate response to her wounding, it was the source of energy for her to change and undertake her own healing.

It is most difficult to get through anger when we acknowledge that we ourselves are the problem, that we live our lives in bad faith. Surely one of the most shocking discoveries made by those who seek to become conscious and responsible is the realization of one's unconscious collu-

---

[78] *Norton Anthology of Poetry*, p. 505.

sion. The fearfulness that underlies our defenses, our false self, is difficult enough to take on, as illustrated by Jayne's story. So is the pulling back of our projections, our blaming of others, as Gerald demonstrated. But most difficult of all is facing the fact that we perpetuate our own wounding. St. Paul said, though we know the good we do not do the good. A painting by Ivan Albright in the Institute of Art in Chicago is titled, "That Which I Should Have Done I Did Not Do."

Who does not know the bitter salt of these words? Who has not awakened at four a.m. to an encounter with the terrible truth that, history aside, we are to blame for what we have made of our life, for what we have become, for what we have done to others? We may experience these recognitions shamefully, with sadness or depression, but there is also a measure of self-directed anger there.

Sometimes this anger works its way out to manifest in an irascibility with others, even hurtful acts against them. More often, this deep anger, which arises from a soul divided against itself, is directed against ourselves in the thousand denigrations, the self-abuse, the self-destructive acts, the undercutting of one's own potential.

In the end, we must recognize that just as there is a pool of sadness in everyone, so there is a mountain of anger. Anger is a legitimate reaction of the soul to its wounding. We may keep it unconscious precisely because its expression today reactivates the peril its expression once risked. We may turn it upon ourselves by somatizing, depressing or damaging ourselves through our contaminated decisions. Or we may transfer this anger to others, thereby wounding those who are the silent surrogates for those we could not confront in the past. Anger, then, is a reflexive response to the constriction of the soul. As such, it is not only part of the defense system of the psyche, it is a vital intimation which, when tracked, may lead to the soul's healing.

When transformed by consciousness, anger becomes vital energy which is available not only for healing but also for furthering the desires of the soul. As long as we are wound-identified, we remain stuck in our victimage, up to our ears in the sour soup of wrath. When we can acknowledge that our road may be blocked by the triple-headed Cerberus, the mad dog of too-much-ness, too-little-ness and self-hatred, then it becomes possible to pass by his growling grasp.

While original wounds can rarely be healed, what they have come to mean to us symbolically can be reshaped. When we are stuck in anger, however legitimate it may be, we are mired in Hell, in the lower regions of our history. Our present life is still defined by that past wounding. When we can acknowledge anger, track its origin, see its effect on our imaginal self, then at last we may break free of the limits of the past. The three-headed Cerberus seems to be on the path, out there, ahead of us, blocking our way. But he is inside; we carry him. When we acknowledge with Dr. Faustus that where we are is Hell, we have already begun the long road up and out of the nether kingdom.

7
Fear and Anxiety

Angst the Iceberg, We the Titanic

As I begin this chapter my daughter Taryn is having contractions every five minutes. By the time I finish this chapter I hope to have seen my daughter and met my first grandchild, Rachel. I look forward to this double pleasure. I also have to confess to a neurotic thought.

The moment I was told that Rachel was on her way I experienced angst, not joy. My first thought, and I am not proud of it, was, "Someone else to worry about." My second thought was for Taryn and the new burdens that she, a career woman, would soon be carrying. My third thought was the "right" one—a deep sense of awe at the great movement of nature of which we are such a tiny but momentous part. I recalled being present at Taryn's birth and not believing the miracle I was experiencing, nor since can I believe the grace that has come my way from knowing her. So, too, the birth of her brother, Timothy, about the most interesting person I have ever met. Blessed as I have been by such wonderful children, now grown-ups and friends, why my first neurotic, angst-ridden thought?

There is a thread running beneath everything we have encountered so far in this book. There is, for all the variety of the swampland states, an element common to all. That common thread is angst. I label my initial reaction to my daughter's pregnancy as neurotic, and I will take responsibility for that. But my reaction was clearly reflexive in nature, outside my conscious will and desire. Why, then, in the midst of something wondrous and transcendent, would one feel this undercurrent, this pull down into a dismal swampland?

Martin Heidegger has called our species, in one of those German portmanteau words, the "Being-toward-Death." Soren Kierkegaard wrote eloquently about "fear and trembling" in a book of that name. And W.H. Auden called our time "The Age of Anxiety."

In *Tracking the Gods* I suggest that entire generations may be anxious

101

if the mythological carpet is pulled from beneath their feet. The steady erosion of stabilizing mythologies has dimmed the inner longitudes and latitudes from which humans have drawn their bearings for centuries. Without rehearsing the evidence for what led our world from the dour certainties of Dante to the baleful vision of Samuel Beckett, we may all agree that cultural values have become less clear and traditional institutions less comforting. While much freedom for innovation and creativity may derive from such loss, few of us feel thankful to live "between two worlds, / one dead, the other powerless to be born."[79]

Taryn's contractions continue as I write. Rachel's reluctance to come into this world is understandable. Why should anyone leave such a sinecure, such a safe house, for this perilous place? That little girl may be smarter than the rest of us, but she cannot, in the end, avoid being human. Which makes her one of us. She will fall from the timeless into history, from innocence into guilt, and from *participation mystique* into alienation. She will be one of us, and then, when she is grown and reading this, perhaps forgive her long-departed grandfather for his "neurotic" thoughts on the night of her sacred transit into the world.

But what accounts for that thread running beneath all behaviors? Connected once to the heartbeat of the cosmos, all needs met, we fall into a perilous condition. Our birth is traumatic, a psychic wounding, a catastrophic event from which we never fully recover. Most of life's motifs arise in response to this cataclysmic separation. Either we seek to return to the umbilical state, or we are obliged to seek connections in the uncertain world around us. Since we cannot literally return to the womb, the regressive identification with the mother finds cultural form in our remaining psychologically infantile, in our effort to blur painful consciousness through drugs and alcohol, or in relinquishing our developmental tasks by turning them over to some guru or cult.

We all have these regressive tendencies. In the past they were overcome by supportive rites of passage providing the momentum and enlarged values through which libido was transformed from regression to progression. Today, without meaningful rites of passage, without cul-

---

[79] Matthew Arnold, "Stanzas from 'The Grand Chartreuse,' " in ibid., p. 794.

turally meaningful mythologies, we are generally obliged to make the break alone, as best we can. What dogs our every developmental step is increased anxiety. As a matter of fact, we are daily obliged to choose between anxiety and depression. If we are caught in regressive behaviors, thereby sabotaging our individuation, we will suffer depression. If we overthrow our psychic lethargy and move out into the world, we will experience an increase of anxiety. Hardly a pretty choice, but it is a choice we make, consciously or not, virtually every moment.

It may be useful to differentiate the differences between *fear, anxiety* and *angst.* Fear is specific. We fear dogs because we were once bitten. Anxiety is a free-floating dis-ease which may be activated by nearly anything, may even light for a while on something specific, but which usually originates from the general insecurity one feels in one's life. The level of that insecurity, the amount of anxiety that may be tapped, is partly a function of one's particular history. The more troubled one's environment, family of origin and cultural setting, the more free-floating anxiety will be generated. The nature and character of the trauma one has suffered will similarly vary from person to person. Angst, on the other hand, is present in us all, a function of the fragile human condition. One might define angst as existential anxiety; that is, it comes from being an animal who can become conscious of just how thin the thread by which it hangs really is.

A poem by M. Truman Cooper illustrates the various ways in which fear, anxiety and angst intermingle and begin to feel like the same thing:

> Suppose that what you fear
> could be trapped,
> and held in Paris.
> Then you would have
> the courage to go
> everywhere in the world.
> All the directions of the compass
> open to you,
> except the degrees east or west
> of true north
> that lead to Paris.
> Still, you wouldn't dare
> put your toes

smack dab on the city limit line.
You're not really willing
to stand on a mountainside
miles away,
and watch the Paris lights
come up at night.
Just to be on the safe side,
you decide to stay completely
out of France.
But then danger
seems too close
even to those boundaries,
and you feel
the timid part of you
covering the whole globe again.
You need the kind of friend
who learns your secret and says,
"See Paris first."[80]

If one takes the image of Paris literally, fear of the city as such seems absurd. If one had had a traumatic experience in Paris, however, the mere mention of the name could stir a large affect. But we know the poet is using Paris as a metaphor for what we fear. The name could just as easily be Zürich or Toronto, or one's home town. The fear of Paris begins to edge over into the anxiety we carry at all times, the nonspecific fears. Paris goes where we go; we may not be sure we have not blundered across some city line somewhere. All roads lead not to Rome but to Paris, not the City of Light but the City of Existential Angst.

Even when we have absented ourselves from the things that bring us fear, Paris follows us; Paris is everywhere. "Which way I flee is me; myself am Paris," as Milton might have written. Since Paris cannot be avoided, the only constructive possibility is to face and go through what we fear, in order to depotentiate its tyranny over us. The "friend" who says "See Paris first" is the voice of the Self, the inner regulating center which seeks our healing. Cooper knows a swampland when he sees one; he also knows the only way we can go through such a dismal place.

---

[80] "Fearing Paris," p. 64.

We owe the development of what we call depth psychology to the omnipresence of anxiety and its myriad manifestations—"neurosis." When Charcot and Janet, Freud, Breuer and Jung ran up against the limits of the medical model, they were driven to start looking for the invisible forces that refused to respond to potions, nostrums or surgeries.

Initially, they were led into the recesses of the psyche by the many cases of what was then called "hysteria," later "conversion neurosis," and now "somatoform disorder." These disturbances of the body did not seem to derive from any biological etiology, nor, in most cases, did they seem to be symptoms of malingering. But the impairment to the individual was clearly substantial.

While Freud was influenced by many tributaries, it was his genius to discern that the symptomatology was a compromise formation in which two values, sometimes opposing values, were served. If as a child I feel anxious about an upcoming math exam, I can get a genuine headache from the constricted capillaries such stress causes me. I have a headache, certainly, but I also may plead illness and miss the exam. For the small price of a headache I can avoid Paris.

I first encountered a somatoform neurosis during my analytic training. Lily had an overwhelming mother complex. Her mother was invasive, devouring and narcissistic. She had managed to sabotage every relationship Lily had ever attempted. Lily remained depressed and angry in this involuntary servitude but could not escape her mother's powerful spell. Periodically Lily would experience paralysis in her left arm, roughly from the elbow down. Neurological tests revealed nothing. Since the paralysis only affected her sporadically, and then for perhaps half an hour or so, she tended to dismiss its importance.

On one occasion, three months into her analysis (which she kept secret from her mother), Lily experienced the paralysis in a session. Our conversation about it led nowhere. As the session ended, I tossed her a pen so she could make a note of her next appointment. She deftly caught the pen with her left hand and I realized for the first time that she was left-handed. "What would you do with that arm," I asked her in that moment which had briefly opened to her interior. "I'd kill her," she said, with a stabbing motion of the pen.

In the next session we talked about the quantity of homicidal emotion she carried, and how such energy, expressed or not, was toxic to her and those around her. Lily was able to acknowledge the rage hiding beneath her depression; nevertheless, two weeks later she attacked her mother, strangled her within an inch of her life and pulled some of her hair out.

Shocked by what she had done, Lily moved out of her mother's house. Even the early warning could not prevent her rage from surfacing. Lily's repressed anger was so great that it made her anxious, though she did not consciously appreciate the level of energy, as Fritz Zorn had not, until too late. Her paralysis occurred when homicidal thoughts nudged her. But those thoughts occasioned so much anxiety that she could not assimilate it and the energy got shuttled off into the venue of the body. Indeed, the level of anxiety tapped into by this violent episode so frightened Lily that she also stopped her analysis.

In this example we may observe the fine line between anxiety, deriving from a profound crippling complex, and angst, the ambivalent lot of everyone who must separate from the parents. Maturation inevitably requires progressive separations, any one of which may occasion anxiety as one leaves the familiar for the foreign, but in Lily's case the power of legitimate angst was multiplied by the power of anxiety specific to her mother complex.

Phobias (from the Greek *phobos,* meaning "fear") may be occasioned by a specific trauma. It would seem reasonable to acquire a flight phobia if one witnessed an airplane crash. But often phobias are not based on any identifiable traumatic experience.

Many times the object of our fear is a symbolic representation for the anxiety that floats unnamed in the unconscious. Agoraphobia, for example, in Greek means "fear of the marketplace," a puzzling malady if taken literally. What characterizes the "marketplace," however, is its openness, the likelihood of running into others, the unpredictable, in other words the loss of control one risks by venturing outside the safety of home.

One woman, an artist by talent and a bank clerk by profession, had a special fear of heights. She heroically worked with her acrophobia over a period of several months by taking an elevator to increasingly higher floors, and walking to the end window in order to stare out over the city. While this desensitizing was helpful, the deeper work in the analysis took its bearing from that anxiety we all share when we encounter the largeness of the journey ahead. What her phobia symbolized was the loss of grounding implicit in openly exploring her talent; she feared her own heights and depths, the risk inherent in daring to believe in herself. To act on her vocational summons would be to step out, unsupported, into psychic space. Thus, the thing feared may have its origin in a trauma, but it also often, or instead, symbolizes some deeper anxiety we have not made conscious, or perhaps some task we have not found the strength to take on. Such "fear," ironically, is a defense against anxiety, which in turn may be a defense against angst.

Anxiety which is not made conscious is most pernicious, for we can never know exactly where it will go, and it will always go somewhere—into a projection or into the body. Under the fetid roof of repression breed foul monsters who will, inevitably, break forth from their fetters in some other venue. Many times the anxiety will be displaced, as in the above examples of phobias. Eating disorders are rife today, particularly among young and middle-aged women. As we saw earlier in the chapter on obsessions and addictions, what obsesses one not only obliges a narrowing of consciousness but an effort to manage anxiety. Thus the anorexic or bulimic focuses on body image and/or food, for such seems something over which they may exercise a measure of control. One can, apparently, choose what enters the narrow choke point of the mouth, thereby controlling *something* when everything else in one's life seems out of control. Thus, an eating disorder is not only a narrowing of the range of one's conscious life but an overcompensation for anxiety.

Cynthia had lost both her parents while she was a child. She grew up in the care of a reluctant relative who offered control and admonition but little love. As an adolescent Cynthia turned to kleptomania, stealing tokens of worth for herself in lieu of affection bestowed. She also began binging and purging on chocolate. As an adult in therapy, she had recurrent nightmares of losing her teeth, which symbolically constituted the first line of defense for her. Similarly, she dreamt of enemies creeping across the borders while guards slept at their posts. On the one hand, through binging on chocolate, she gave herself something sweet when life had only presented her with sourness. On the other hand, she reasserted control over her overwhelming anxiety by purging the sweet sin of her chocomania.

Cynthia's wound was that of abandonment. No one had ever really been there for her, and this experience generated an enormous amount of anxiety. At the same time, the deprivation of parental love and support rippled through the child's sensibility and occasioned archetypal wounding. As the personal parent is the mediator of the world, of the body, of relationship, determining the particular valence of the complex, so too the parent triggers the archetypal extrapolation and thereby begets an existential angst.

For Cynthia, the lack of loving parents resulted in more than a powerful complex; it was a wounding introduction to the whole world. Her "choice" of an eating disorder is similarly both a personal complex which defends against anxiety, and an archetypal strategy which defends against angst. As the loss of a nurturing mother activates the negative mother complex, so the control of the concomitant angst focuses on the *Mater*-matter-food-body nexus. To be abandoned in a motherless universe is an unbearable horror; better to worry about food intake instead. What I can then worry about, be preoccupied by, is a defense against what I fear would obliterate me. My neurosis is a primitive, primal defense against insupportable angst. Painful as it is, it is preferable to the totally unbearable.

When the true terror floats near the surface, it is easily activated and one may be subject to panic attacks. Few states are more chilling, for during the endless minutes this state lasts, one feels one is literally dying. There are bodily sensations of choking, shortness of breath or palpitations of the heart, the sense of being completely overwhelmed. We flounder in the trackless forest of the unconscious. This is the goat-footed guy's domain, Pan's place, and we panic.

A proclivity to panic may have a biological basis, as current fragmentary evidence suggests. It is also true that we may learn such behavior from observing parents or other authority figures being overwhelmed. But a panic attack may also derive from a displacement of the unthinkable onto the local. If I focus on my big toe long enough it will begin to hurt, and before long I can come to believe that the pain heralds some terminal illness. The experience of hypochondria is an easy escalation from a normal concern about health. One cannot argue that there is no cancer, no heart attack, no death. And yet the preoccupation with health is somehow preferable to an encounter with the even bigger horror that anything can and might happen. Hypochondria at least offers a sense of control, of potential healing. It is easier to seek some elusive cause than conjure with the truth: that one will die, that one is not in control of the universe. Rather than catastrophize consciously, and bear it, we catastrophize unconsciously and suffer the attacks of rampant emotions.

The "going through" of a panic disorder, or indeed any anxiety state, obliges us to consciously catastrophize, that is, look at the terrible reality. When we do so we find we can, as adults, bear it, even find a measure of acceptance and, once in awhile, the ability to let go. Alternatively, not letting go means that when we next, inadvertently but unavoidably, stray off the narrow path, we will again find ourselves in Pan's woods. Like the alligators who once lurked beneath our childhood beds, or the monsters who hid in the closet, we know he is there, the little goat-guy with cloven hoofs; we know he is coming to get us.

As noted in the chapter on obsessions and addictions, we are all prone to repetitive behavior in angst-laden situations. We may not notice that in the face of stress we fidget in a certain fashion, mumble a pat phrase, pray without reflection. Even the phrase "to get out of bed on the wrong side" intimates the routinization of life, not only because daily schedules may replicate themselves, but because we often unconsciously organize our existence according to the unconscious dictates of magical thinking.

Magical thinking is a characteristic of children, so-called primitive cultures and also ourselves when we are regressed, vulnerable. Through magical thinking we can convince ourselves that our thoughts and behavior have a special causal effect on the world, just as the world has a secret causal effect on us. We observe superstitions half-consciously. An athlete on a winning streak may wear the same dirty socks for each game until the string is broken. Entertainers are told to "break a leg" lest good wishes invoke the wrath of the gods. I still catch myself trying not to step on cracks, to save my mother's back.

We all, unconsciously, contrive ritualized behavior to ward off dark, nebulous forces. When our rituals fail to work, we feel a heightened angst. We become furious that the newspaper didn't arrive on time, that we left a certain object behind, or that we have to change our usual path to work. These rituals are magical talismen against the unbearable thought that we are in an alien and not always friendly universe. Our rituals are fragile stays against the ocean of angst and, tenuous though they be, we cling to them.

In a full-blown obsessive-compulsive disorder, the person has unconsciously "chosen" recurrent thoughts and behaviors as a ritualized defense against the overwhelming sea of angst. New antidepressants have shown some secondary effect in reducing the intensity of obsessional thinking. But we all have thoughts we don't wish to have. Under the defense of any obsession lies an enormous angst. What I can bear to look at directly may give me an unpleasant time, but it no longer owns me.

Occasionally we choose what is euphemistically called the "advantage of illness," or the "secondary gain" of neurosis. With a "factitious disorder," we may invent or feign a physical or psychological malady. Our distress allows us to assume the role of the afflicted, perhaps avoid other stressful demands, and thus finesse our way out of greater anxieties. If I am obese I may not have to suffer the task and nuances of relationship. I may lament my lot and kvetch about the insensitivity of others toward me, but I manage to stay within the fortification of my body. If I am disabled I am surely not obliged to belly up to the bar of life and take more hits. In acquiescing to my anxiety I avoid a larger measure of angst.

All behaviors, even those we dub "crazy," are logical when seen as an expression of, or reaction to, a certain emotional premise. That is why, in the analytic detection of etiology, one has to ask the question, "What emotional state could generate this behavior?" No matter how symbolically disguised, visible symptoms dramatize an unconscious affective premise. This causal relationship between affective state and symbolic expression has a cyclic effect and in time becomes not only an expression of a particular wound but also a generalized personality form and strategy. We become our wounds, so to speak. We live out those reactions which come from the fated wounding and thereby collude with the symbolic expressions. This assemblage of behaviors, attitudes and reflexive strategies constitutes our "false self," a provisional personality. Thus we are trapped not only in our wounds but in our reactions to them. Not permitted by fate to unfold naturally, we are obliged to experience ourselves in reactive patterns that progressively estrange us from ourselves.

The result of self-estrangement is neurosis. Unavoidable as neurosis may be—and indeed, even preferable to remaining unconscious—the only antidote, the only way out, is to face what the neurosis is a defense against. What task are we avoiding? There is always a task.

Managing Anxiety

Our most primitive defense is the familiar "fight or flight" option. What we find overwhelming we usually flee from. We learn to distance ourselves from painful realities. "Out of sight, out of mind." "What you don't know won't hurt you." We repress, we forget, we split off; we project our unpleasant complexes onto others. We may serve our dissociated complexes for decades and never become conscious of their infernal underground work. When they possess us, we are transported to another frame of reference and operate within that frame, slipping back into ordinary consciousness without even noticing the shift.

Dissociative states may manifest relatively harmlessly in the daily repression of unpleasant truths; we all do that and are none the worse for that. But dissociation may be more profound; it can result in amnesia or a "fugue" state, in which one literally forgets one's identity and wanders about in someone else's biography. The multiple personality disorder (today called Dissociative Identity Disorder) has gained a great deal of notoriety in recent years, the subject of some sensational legal cases as well as great controversy within therapeutic circles.

In a dissociative identity disorder the ego has taken such a battering that it cannot hold its own against the unconscious; then the psyche shifts automatically to an alternative reality. This is also a normal phenomenon, which is why Jung defined a complex as "a splinter personality."[81] But in

---

[81] "A Review of the Complex Theory," *The Structure and Dynamics of the Psyche,* CW 8, par. 97.

extreme cases such a psychic fragment may have a biography quite unknown by the ego, and a concomitant somatic and affective state. In the presence of great trauma, we all manage the unacceptable level of anxiety by depersonalization. We detach ourselves, may feel as if we are looking on our own lives as an observer. Sometimes this distancing, this detachment, is essential to getting through an experience. It is only pathological if the depersonalization persists unduly beyond the event.

Two other categories of reflexive response to anxiety require noting: adjustment disorders and personality disorders.

Adjustment disorders are usually directly linked to stressors and may employ any tools available, such as avoidance, perfectionism as a defense against the anxiety of incompleteness, or the whole range of somatic and affective symptoms of anxiety. Generally, when the stress is relieved, the disorder wanes.

In the case of the personality disorder, the person has almost always been an early victim of significant trauma, such as emotional, physical or sexual abuse. When the fragile boundaries of the child are overrun, when the ego cannot cope with the overwhelming flood of emotion, something shuts down. Like a surge-suppressor on a computer, the personality breaks the connection lest it be repeatedly, and painfully, overloaded. While this response is, again, quite logical given the etiology, the feeling function generally remains permanently disabled. Such persons often experience life from a distance, as if watching themselves in a movie. They usually have a history of poor relationships, as the ability to empathize with the other when the relationship inevitably makes emotional demands has been profoundly eroded.

Thus the paranoid personality, having suffered "betrayal" from the primal objects, mother and father, will organize the personality to expect and to find such betrayal everywhere. Being programmed to betrayal, such a person will unwittingly choose partners who play out the unconscious script, or the suspicions, the control, the inability to trust, will drive the partner away—thereby confirming one's first thought not to invest trustingly in the relationship.

The schizoid personality disorder is an act of overprotection. Such a person detaches from others, offers only a limited range of feeling response and tends to avoid intimate relationships. This self-defeating behavior does achieve its goal, namely to protect against having to reexperience the painful wounding of the past. The antisocial personality, having been wounded early as well, sees others as enemies to be used, lest they use one first. The betrayal of the primal relationships is extrapolated to include society in general; not only is the feeling function shut down, so that one registers very little personal pain or remorse, but the former victim now victimizes others.

The borderline personality disorder is most characterized by the instability of object relationships because that person's own self-image is unstable. Often this person acts impulsively, with little regard for damage to others, suffers profound shifts of mood, and is haunted by chronic feelings of emptiness. Again, the effect of overwhelming anxiety in childhood has created such a fragile sense of self that behavioral continuity is virtually impossible to achieve.

The histrionic personality disorder is based on the child's untended need for attention, love and approval. Thus, this person is agitated when not the center of attention; he or she speaks and acts in ways that draw attention, and suffers fits of jealousy and rage at real or imagined slights. Similarly, the narcissistic personality disorder is often a real pain to others. Such a person manages the huge anxiety of self-doubt by demanding admiration and reassurance, feeling entitled to special treatment from others and yet lacking empathy for the needs and suffering of others. They are hard to take because of their need to control others, but for all their outer display of bravado, inwardly they feel empty and unloved. They are only able to carry on sustained relations with dependent or codependent persons who will agree to orbit their lives around the empty narcissistic ego.

Dependent personality disorders and obsessive-compulsive personality disorders seem polarities. The former manages the quanta of anxiety by avoidance of decisions and commitments, extreme deference and surrender of personal integrity in order to receive crumbs from the other's table. The obsessive-compulsive, on the other hand, responds to the ambiguities of life by exercising a heightened effort to control, operating out of anxious urgency all the time. Such people are preoccupied with details so that the larger picture is forgotten; they are workaholics, overly conscientious and miserly in giving affection to themselves or others.

What is so intractable about personality disorders is that the damage to the soul usually occurred to the fragile, vulnerable child, whose nascent ego was understandably unable to process this traumatic experience and shut down the vital feeling function which otherwise helps one to evaluate and respond qualitatively to life. Similarly, the natural personality is greatly skewed, and the person becomes locked into a pathologized, and often pathologizing, strategy for life. Sadly, therapy is seldom sought by them for they would be obliged to face the childhood terrors they are defending against.

When someone with a personality disorder does seek therapy, the work of healing is extraordinarily difficult because of that person's resistance, and sometimes inability, to internalize. The ability to really acknowledge what one is feeling, and take responsibility for it, is the prime index of whether a person can find healing in therapy or in relationship. Again, one is asked to do what feels impossible, to take on the large hurt and stand in a feeling relationship to it. Occasionally healing does occur, not from any interpretation or intervention by the therapist, but because of the consistency and continuity of a caring relationship, the one thing the child did not experience. Such a reformation of the sense of self, of the experience of the other, and of the reflexive traffic between, requires years of patience.

While personality disorders are the most difficult therapeutic dilemmas, the task remains the same here as elsewhere: to "go through," to meet the anxiety head-on and break its tyranny. But it is not easy to bear this primal anxiety and to risk departing from the personality structure we evolved in order to survive in the first place. The more overwhelming the primal experience, the more extensive the damage to the ego and thus the more formidable the task.

Variants of the above-mentioned strategies for, and reflexive responses to, the management of anxiety may be found in all of us. It is only a matter of the depth and systemization of such responses. The more primal and reflexive such patterns are, the more we are their prisoners. Fears are normal and natural. Anxiety, which is a function of our personal history, is normal and natural. Angst, which is a consequent of the fragility of the human condition, is also normal and natural. What varies is the degree of affect and the nature and consequences of our responses. Since each of us has evolved reflexive responses to this anxiety, so we are in some profound and often unconscious ways prisoners of our own history. As our history and its responses remain powerfully programmed, whether we are conscious of this dynamic or not, so we collude in our repetitive wounding. "Which way I flee is me; myself am Hell."

There is an essential difference between normal anxiety and anxiety that is neurotically crippling. To live fully in the world is to frequently suffer the bouts of anxiety that are our lot as a sentient species. We should never deride ourselves for such anxiety. It becomes a psychological problem only when we are prevented by that anxiety from living our lives as fully as possible. And it becomes a moral problem when our own chosen strategies impair and impede us. So we are anxious? . . . so we are still obliged to live as fully as possible. One thinks of the epitaph Nikos Kazantzakis wrote for himself, "I want nothing. I fear nothing. I am free."[82] A difficult but worthwhile goal.

Anxiety is the price of a ticket on the journey of life; no ticket—no journey; no journey—no life. We may run from anxiety as much as possible but we thereby run from our only life. Just as Freud noted that the task of therapy is to move one from neurotic miseries to the normal miseries of life, so we are impelled to face what we cannot face, bear what we cannot bear, name the unnamable that haunts us.

Again, we are daily forced to choose between depression and anxiety. Depression results from the wounding of the individuation imperative; anxiety results from moving forward into the unknown. The path of anxiety is necessary because therein lies the hope of the person to more nearly become an individual. My analyst once said to me, "You must make your fears your agenda." When we do take on that agenda, for all the anxiety engendered, we feel better because we know we are living in *bonne foi* with ourselves.

Courage is not the absence of fear. It is the perception that some

---

[82] *The Saviors of God,* p. 134.

things are more important to us than what we fear. The individuation task, for example, is more important than whatever regressively blocks us. Interestingly enough, we make a great move toward personal liberation when we can acknowledge the existential angst directly, know ourselves to be fragile beings clinging to a spinning planet hurtling through space, and at the same time be grateful for such a grand ride. We gain when we are able to move from the anxiety which, like fog, obscures the forward path. When, in that cloud, we can identify specific fears, we will often find them groundless to us as adults, though they were once overwhelming to the child. If, for example, one has an inordinate fear of conflict, and avoids speaking at meetings, one needs to find the discrete fear in the cloud of paralyzing anxiety. Generally, such an anxious thought will translate into an early fear, such as, "They won't approve, " "They won't love me."

These primal fears were real for the child, but the adult we have become can have a different experience. What I can make conscious, face directly and deal with as an adult, frees me from unconscious bondage to the past. We truly perceive that something is more important than what we fear. And there is. *We* are more important than what we fear. This is what is meant by courage.

And now my dear granddaughter Rachel Erin, seven pounds and nine ounces, she of the puff-cheeks and eyes to die for, crying lustily for food and the place to which she can never return, is among us. With puff-cheeks and eyes to die for she begins her wondrous, angst-laden journey toward her destiny. How much she, and the rest of us, can move through fate toward destiny will be a function of how much life we can seize in the face of the angst that remains our most constant companion.

8
A Simple Complex Interlude

Before looking at the question of working with swampland states, we need to review for a moment Jung's theory of complexes. Much has been written about them elsewhere, so we will not tarry long. However, the idea of the complex is important for us in this context.

If Jung had died before 1912, when he articulated his theory of the archetypes and the collective unconscious, he would still be important as the one who discovered the existence of complexes. In fact, before he began calling his approach "analytical psychology" in order to differentiate it from Freud's school of "psychoanalysis," Jung called his work "complex psychology" because of the importance of complexes in his model of the psyche. Indeed, in his introductory lectures on psychoanalysis Freud gave credit to Jung and the so-called Zürich school for the idea of complexes as the architects of dreams.

Jung was led to the idea of complexes from a number of tributaries. I will mention only two. His medical dissertation was an investigation of a medium whose somnambulistic utterances had fascinated him.[83] She was a relative whose sincerity he trusted. How then to account for the "voices" that came through her? She was not psychotic and hallucinating. While he considered it possible that there might be phantasms, presences from another world, he came to the conclusion that the medium was able to reduce her ego control to an extremely labile state and allow the different parts of herself to speak. (This occurs to us all as we dream.)

Secondly, in his research on word association at the Burgholzli Klinik in Zürich in the first decade of this century, he found that even normal people experienced disturbances of attention in their responses to words. It seemed as if the stimulus word triggered an affective charge sufficient to interfere with the intention of consciousness.[84] In time Jung speculated

---

[83] See "On the Psychology and Pathology of So-Called Occult Phenomena," *Psychiatric Studies,* CW 1.
[84] See "The Association Method," *Experimental Researches,* CW 2.

that there were clusters of split-off energy in us all, and these clusters he called *complexes.*

A complex as such is merely an energized structure. The valency of such charged energy may be positive, negative or mixed, depending on its impact in our life. Complexes are generated by our history. We cannot avoid them because we are never free of our history. In fact, it seems that everything that has ever happened to us is still alive somewhere in the depths of our psyche. The more primal the experience, the more powerful the complex. Thus, because of our sensitivity as children, the parental complexes are usually the most influential in our psychological makeup.

Normally we do not know we are acting out of a complex because when one is activated it has the power to take over consciousness. Try telling a person possessed by a complex that they are in one. They will deny it and insist on the validity of their perception. We may only come to recognize the presence of complexes after the fact, after they have done damage. Or we may begin to recognize their activation when we feel a somatic shift, since such energy always affects the body. A certain chilling of the extremities, tightening of the throat, sweating palms and so on are clues that the split-off material has been activated.

Secondly, we may recognize a complex because of the affect generated. When we feel ourselves "charged up" we may tumble to the fact that we are in the grip of a complex. Even then, the work of understanding it and reducing its unwanted power often lasts a lifetime.

The diagram opposite illustrates the dynamics of a complex. When we hit our swampland states, with all their negative affects, we are likely to respond in patterned ways. If we are to work with the swamplands, break the tyranny of the past, we are obliged to understand this process.

There are three levels of psychic reality depicted in the diagram: the conscious life or outer world, the personal unconscious, which is the sum of the emotional history of the individual, and the archetypal ground or collective unconscious, which is where we share common traits, drives and patterns with all humanity, past and present.

The world of the personal unconscious is clustered with affectively charged energies which derive from experience. If we were once bitten by a dog, say, we will have a "dog-bite" complex whether we know it or

COMPLEX CIRCUITRY

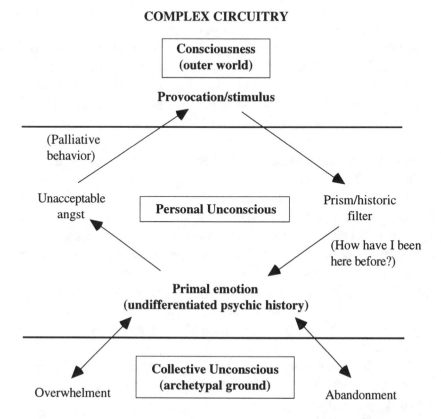

not. And even if we are a lover of dogs because we have also had many positive experiences of them, the dog-bite complex is nonetheless there and may be constellated (activated) by a replication of the earlier experience or by an analogous experience.

The charged clusters are buttons, so to speak, which we unavoidably make available to the world and which may be unwittingly pressed by anyone at any time. The more intimate a relationship, the more buttons are liable to be pressed since we are closer to the primal intimacy, the parent-child relationship. For this reason, close relationships are inevitably saddled with the burden of past wounds and unrealistic expectations. This is not fair to our partners, of course, but it is unavoidable.

Virtually anything in the outer world—a chance encounter, a smell, a song on the radio, a face in the street—may provoke the activation of unconscious energy. The stimulus is immediately passed through a prism of sorts, an historic filter which asks the implicit question, "How have I been here before?" The immediate stimulus may be unique, but the psyche is nothing if not a charged history and so seeks the analogue. When we visit a foreign country we seek to make ourselves comfortable by groping for words or customs familiar to us, in order to reduce our anxiety in the presence of the unknown. We can fall into great difficulty, whether in a foreign culture or at home, by responding reflexively to the present out of our analogous past.

The early Greeks felt that we often make choices injurious to ourselves and others because of some flaw in our character, the *hamartia,* our way of seeing the world. It is not that we are evil or deliberately perverse, but we do tend to act self-destructively, repeating our patterns and suffering the consequences. This *hamartia* is a sort of psychic prism acquired by our phenomenological "reading" of the world. As an amalgam of our experience of our family of origin, our cultural context and personal wounding, it leads us to see the world in a biased fashion. It is the filter through which we see ourselves and others, and the basis of our repetitive, historically analogous choices. Obviously, we will be forever subject to the narrowness of that focus unless we make it conscious and broaden our perspective.

Charged personal complexes resonate throughout the psyche and activate the primal emotions we have never been able to assimilate. This undifferentiated psychic history includes all that was larger than the child's sensibility could process. Obviously, we have many more capacities than those represented by the child's vision, but even the adult can be overwhelmed by the immense influx of daily experience. Here the complexes unique to the individual are the bridges, however, to the archetypal experience of the race. As we experienced our mother, our father, for example, so they, as bridges to the larger world, are sustained by us as charged complexes which then activate the archetypal ground. Central to this primal material are the twin wounds of overwhelment or abandonment. More than mother and father, we carry a deep sensibility and perception about how generally nurturing or hostile this universe is. So, too, any complex has roots which reach deeply down into the ground of Being itself. As our personal material is activated, so ripples reach the resonant reservoir wherein we participate in all of nature.

The activation of negatively charged complexes, and their resonance into the precarious reaches of nature, are always attended by anxiety and angst, whether we are conscious of this in the moment or not. Anxiety and angst are discomfiting, unacceptable; we reflexively engage in some form of behavior to palliate our discomfort. The range of such behaviors runs the gamut from fight to flight, from dissociation and denial, to obsessive-compulsive caretaking and co-dependence. In the course of our life we may try many possibilities, and over time we develop certain routine strategies and responses to stressful situations. Unwittingly, we become prisoners of history, prisoners of ourselves.

Complex circuitry is akin to an electric circuit. A switch is turned and a light goes on in no time. Similarly, the stimulus, the prism processing, the activation of archaic material, the evocation of angst and the palliative behavior that completes the circuit may transpire in a fraction of a second. Without warning we are no longer in the moment but back in the long corridors of history, at the site of our primal memories, and beyond. And all we may have been aware of was a sudden *frisson*.

Since we pride ourselves on our consciousness and maturity, it is deeply disturbing to think how much of our lives is driven autonomously by our history-based patterns, buried so deeply that we may never know of their existence or silent control. But the existence of complexes does go a long way toward explaining why relationships are difficult, why we so often get in our own way, and why the world is always a mess.

We can never fully know what historically conditioned forces shape and direct us. Even the complexes we become conscious of often resist all our efforts to depotentiate them. The circuitry of some is so deeply wired as to be part of our mainframe, and no change of floppy disk can override our conditioned response. Working with a complex is not unlike trying to free an old mill horse. For all its life it has pulled the great mill stone around and around its grinding circuit. We unharness it, read it a bill of rights and awake the next morn to see the old fellow walking the same rutted circle.

I think of Patrick, who grew up with an emotionally invasive mother. She dominated his life, constricted his emotional life and in general suppressed his natural development. He "escaped" her tyranny by marrying the same kind of woman. Decades later, his life is dominated in every way by his wife. He risks no opinion, makes hardly a move, without first checking it out with her. Talk about the frying pan and the fire.

Throughout his life Patrick has suffered from depression, which for some years he tried to medicate with alcohol. Also, and paradoxically one might think, for many years Patrick has had a mistress in another city. Periodically he drives for three hours to see her, but he is hardly able to enjoy the tryst because he is so consumed by guilt and deadly fearful of his wife finding out. Like the mill horse he continues sadly in the same depressive circuit. Patrick has a mother complex as big as a house. He can only obey it or, all atremble, react secretly against it. He resists the effort it would take, the heroic effort, to stand up to the complex, take it on and suffer through to achieve his own life.

How may we ever transcend history, patterns so deeply programmed as to seem to be who we are in fact, rather than the internalization of what happened to us? We can never move beyond the bonds of the past until we can say, and suffer through, "I am not what happened to me; I am what I choose to become." How we may navigate the swampland states without simply miring down, repeating our past and wounding ourselves even further, is the subject of our last chapter.

9
Going Through

Behold your thoughts and feelings . . . there stands a mighty ruler, an unknown sage—whose name is Self.—Friedrich Nietzsche.

Truth is always on the side of the more difficult.—Friedrich Nietzsche.

Re-Imagining Ourselves

As one crosses over the border from North Carolina to Virginia one may drive through a long stretch of swamplands called, graphically enough, "The Great Dismal Swamp," or sometimes by locals simply "The Great Dismal." It is interesting to drive through such miasmic muck on a paved road, but no one I know would like to reside there. So, some readers of this book are perhaps thinking, "Very well, how do we avoid these swamplands"? As understandable as such a sentiment might be, such readers are hereby invited to go back to page one and start all over.

The point is that we have no choice but to be pulled into these swamplands, and repeatedly. We would like to believe that if we live with probity and high moral purpose we will be exempt. But remember Job and the message of Ecclesiastes. There is no moral contract which we are able to strike with the universe. We, the Parties of the Second Part, may inscribe such a contract in our secret hopes, but the Party of the First Part refuses to be a signatory to our furtive deals. We may also think that if we undertake a sincere and disciplined analysis we will find the high ground and be able to build our castle there. Instead, we find to our dismay that we fall back into the old places, the familiar swamplands we have always known despite our heroic efforts. The great rhythms of nature, of time and tide, of fate and destiny, and of our own psyche, move their powerful ways quite outside our will.

Psychological growth can indeed bring a measure of insight, some corrective behavior and occasionally even wisdom. We are more likely to become conscious by repeatedly falling into a swamp and then, through the work on ourselves, seeing that the summons, our task, is both to suffer it and to find the meaning buried in the muck and mire. But surely one of the most damaging things we can do is to condemn ourselves for our swampland stays, for being there in the first place—as if knowing better had anything to do with it.

When I suffer an anxiety state I may actually raise the level of my anxiety by judging myself harshly, not to mention how I contaminate my surroundings by continuing apprehension and self-criticism. A wound-identified person remains stuck: "I am an inadequate person because I have these anxiety attacks. It has always been this way, and always will be. I am worthless, hopelessly wounded."

Similar thoughts are common in childhood, so vulnerable are we to the opinions of others, and pockets of this kind, "ideas of reference," remain in all of us. As adults, one of our tasks is to realize that such states occur outside our will or causation, that they are transitory, unavoidable, and above all that it is possible to absorb them and get on with our life. When I suffer anxiety, so I suffer anxiety. I still have my life, my task. Walt Whitman proclaimed, "Do I contradict myself? Very well then I contradict myself. I am large; I contain multitudes."[85] And so do we all.

The sooner I adopt such an attitude, the less the damage to my sense of self. Many persons go about feeling marked, tainted by their experience of the swamplands, not knowing that their neighbors suffer them as well. In time, the acceptance of our periodic descent into the underworld moves us toward that enlargement of soul, that embrace of the polarities of life which we call wisdom. We learn knowledge; we cannot learn wisdom. Wisdom arises through the assimilation of suffering. Suffering assimilated enlarges the personality, brings amplitude to the soul.

In the above discussion of complexes, it was noted that they are like splinter personalities, somatic states with split-off biographies, carrying an affective charge that might anytime erupt in unconscious, reflexive behavior. It is disturbing to consider how much of what we think and do is historically conditioned, beyond our conscious control. It is not easy to live with the awareness of such inner complexity. Like the mill horse released of its burden, we may continue in our same dreary circuit.

---

[85] "Song of Myself," in *Norton Anthology of Poetry,* p. 762.

The difference between a mill horse and us is our imaginal capacity. Each complex, as we have seen, has a splinter Weltanschauung. When we are in the complex—that is, when the energic cluster has been activated and possesses us—we are in that Weltanschauung, a world-view always derived from the past, always limited to original traumatic encounters, and always forcing us to see the world through that limited imaginal lens. The mill horse continues the repetitive round because it cannot escape the confines of its historic conditioning, cannot break that mold. Its imaginal limitations are its fate, and its fate constricts its destiny. So, too, we are limited by our complexes to repeat historic response patterns until such time as we can enlarge our vision of the possible—reimagine ourselves.

In *Thus Spoke Zarathustra* Nietzsche asserted:

> Man is a rope, tied between beast and overman—a rope over an abyss. A dangerous across, a dangerous on-the-way, a dangerous looking-back, a dangerous shuddering and stopping.
>
> What is great in man is that he is a bridge and not an end: what can be loved in man is that he is an *overture* and a *going under.*[86]

The "beast" in us is the mill horse of instinct and blind conditioning. The "overman" is Nietzsche's metaphor for the evolved self, the enlarged soul no longer subject to the limitations of mere nature or history. Paradoxically, we are both the tightrope and the abyss. The abyss is our engulfing existential angst, on the one hand, and also the terrible freedom we embody. This freedom is so "terrible" because it fills us with fear to step out into the largeness of our own journey. The poet Antonio Machado once observed,

> Mankind owns four things
> That are no good at sea—
> Rudder, anchor, oars,
> And the fear of going down.[87]

While it might be terrible out there on the rope above the abyss, that is where we are, so it is no time to look down and scamper back, or freeze

---

[86] "Thus Spake Zarathustra," in *The Portable Nietzsche,* pp. 126f.
[87] "Fourteen Poems," in *Times Alone,* p. 113.

in mid-transit. We are out there on the high wire whether we wish it or not. We were put there. As Pascal noted, it is not a matter of deciding whether or not to set sail; we are already launched.[88]

The crossing over of which Nietzsche speaks is analogous to what I mean by the "going through." The going through is not just hanging on until the swamp's miasma lifts, though that can also become necessary; it is the enlargement of oneself through the identification of the task implicit in each swampland state. When Nietzsche sees us as an "overture," he is considering the imaginal renewal of the sense of self which transcends the historically conditioned limits. When he sees us as a "going under," he means that it is through dying to the limits of the old Weltanschauung that we are freed from the iron wheel of Ixion.

Nietzsche was seeking liberation from the constrictions of the Western tradition into a radical reinvention of the individual. What he intended for the work of culture renewal is first necessary for the renewal of the person who must stand strong against the forces of personal history. Back there lies the fated context, the constricting world view, whose power dominates us. Right here is the terrible freedom to traverse the abyss. On the other side of the abyss is the enlargement of one's soul in which history is dynamically contained but no longer determines our lives. Our familial and cultural experience has heretofore formed the rope upon which we sway and tremble. Our education, exploration of the world, the exemplary models of others and learning from our mistakes take us further out there. And there we are, in the middle, equally far from beginning and end.

What, then, constitutes the rest of the rope over the abyss which we are? It is the imaginative function, the power to re-image ourselves as larger than our history. Again, no one is free who cannot say, with feeling, "I am not what happened to me; I am what I choose to become." "I am not my roles; I am my journey." "I am not my limiting experience; I am the creative power of my potential." Such an effort at re-imagining will not spare us the swamplands, but we will be less contained by them.

The imaginal capacity is critical to our psychic operations because im-

---

[88] *Pensées*, p. 242.

ages carry the energy. In a way, one can say that a complex is itself an imago, one that contains a charge of energy. When that energic cluster is activated it triggers an image of who we are, in what context, and what our bound response must be. We carry such imagos in our body, in the somatic states which express wounding and protest. We carry them in our unconscious life, as we can see in our dreams, fantasies and active imagination. Psychic energy is invisible, but the psyche's way of embodying, of incarnating, that energy is through images. Thus, complexes are historically conditioned images which when not recognized have a regressive influence on us, offering only a very constricted imaginative incarnation. The work of insight, the work of suffering, the work of individuation, has as its goal the enlargement of those constructs, images that move and animate our lives whether we intend them or not.

An example of the limitations of history, the deleterious repetition compulsion, and the imperative to enlarge one's imaginal self may be found in the following case example.

Robert, a forty-five-year-old business administrator, had grown up with a narcissistic mother and a passive father whose example had shown Robert that his task in life was to take care of the wounded woman. In addition, during childhood Robert had suffered a string of traumatic surgeries on his spine. Both the model of his father, and the invasions of the surgeons, persuaded him of his powerlessness in the face of such omnipotent forces. Not only was he powerless to make his own choices, he was doubly programmed to serve the Other, and he often described feeling tied to the hospital gurney as a metaphor for his experience of life. When he married, he chose a woman with a congenital illness whose outbreaks he was obliged to attend. What might seem from a distance as compassion, was in fact a guilt-ridden, historically conditioned passivity in the face of the forces around him.

At midlife Robert fell into a debilitating depression. As noted in an earlier chapter, intrapsychic depression is a portrait of some part of the person's psyche which has been suppressed and is in pain. The whole world of feeling, joy, esprit, had been suppressed throughout Robert's life and in fact he had always carried a "smiling depression." Slowly, imperceptibly, he was pulled into an affair with a colleague, a relationship that had damaging effects at his company. He was obliged to leave his job, and the trauma this occasioned soon led him to leave his marriage as well. Painful as it was to end his marriage, what Robert was leaving was the implicit contract he had struck, unconsciously, with his mother, ratified by his father, to take care of that wounded woman. Leaving his marriage was perhaps the only way Robert could leave the complex that had been formed through his early experience.

After a period of painful readjustment, professional dislocation, money stress and guilt over his failed marriage, Robert moved in with the other woman. The future seemed brighter, less impaired by the baggage of the past. Yet, inexplicably, Robert found himself beset with the old depression, a depression that had receded but not departed. He was prone to feel overwhelmed, hopeless about generating a new business, and in time found himself fighting with his new partner, resentful and wanting to run away altogether.

Unwittingly, the Weltanschauung of the mother-father imago, and his powerlessness in the face of the surgeries, remained hard-wired in the mainframe of Robert's psyche. Soon he was treating his new partner with the passive-aggressive strategies he had seen his father use, had employed himself with his demanding wife, and now reemerged as the strategy of one who feels no power to take his life on directly. His resentment of his new partner seemed misplaced, and he began to sabotage the hopes for change and new life to which they had aspired. Thus in the arenas of work, intimacy and his relationship to himself Robert was back in the old swampland. Which is to say, wherever we travel we find our complexes, for they always travel with us. "Which way I flee is me; myself am Hell."

At that point Robert entered therapy. He felt hopeless and powerless, which was in fact the correct interpretation of his primary complex. It took him awhile to recognize that he had reflexively transferred the power his mother once had in his life to his new partner. This is why he had grown depressed, resentful and passive-aggressive. Who wouldn't, at finding oneself again in the same old swamp? And he had transferred the powerlessness of the frightened child on the gurney to the awesome task of starting over in the business world.

When Robert reached his nadir he had the following dream:

> I am with N. [his partner]. There are two small ponds—one clear, one murky. I am lying in the latter. A man standing nearby fishing in the murky pond pulls five trout out on a pole. I step into the murky pond and quickly begin to sink as if it were quicksand. I slide six feet under and roll on my back and put my arms out horizontally to stabilize myself from sinking further. I am stuck there, holding my breath, feeling the suction pulling me under.

Talk about swamplands, this dream depicts Robert's complete clinical picture. At that moment he felt he was just "treading water," trying to keep from sinking.

When Robert reflected on the images in this dream he came up with some useful associations. He had gone fishing with his father and retained positive memories of this as a bonding experience. He observed that trout would never be in such a turbid pond; they needed flowing, fresh water to survive, yet the fisherman had drawn five trout out of the murk. Robert had moved his Hell with him into the new relationship. N. was there, but he could not move toward her nor could she help him out of his dilemma. One pond is clear, representing the healthy, healing encounter with the unconscious, but for the moment Robert is nearly drowning in the other. His posture, which he likened to crucifixion, reminded him of lying strapped down on the gurney. In fact, he associated it with that moment when the I.V. would be placed in his arm while he waited in terror for the ride to the operating room. Robert fears he will drown in this morass, and is barely holding his own.

Robert's dream is a perfect picture of the effect of the primal complex on one's present life. Facing new choices, he finds himself constricted by the old patterns. His passivity in remaking his life is the limitation of his imaginal powers. While he would have wanted N. to reach in and rescue him, she does not. (If in real life she did, she would have fallen into the mother role and he would be no better off; he must rescue himself.)

Robert has essentially two choices in the dream and in his life: he can gradually sink in the muck until his esprit is extinguished, or he can swim like hell. Moreover, a masculine energy is present which offers another approach, one that hearkens back to his need for empowerment through his father. The man who fishes can both enter the water and remain grounded. He is able to draw forth vital elements from the depths, the fish which may nourish and sustain. And, interestingly, as the wise architect of the dream knew, lively trout may be found even in this dismal swamp by those who look for them.

As we discussed the dream, Robert had the thought that the fisherman in the dream might extend his pole into the six-foot depths (which reminded him of being planted six feet down in a grave) and pull Robert up. But that man represents only the potential for rescue. Robert has to reach up to contact him, which is to say, re-image himself not as the passive, terrified child strapped down, but as the swimmer who can contact the fisherman in himself, the imago of the empowered masculine, who can pull himself out of the swamp, out of the Ixion-repetition of his father's life. This is the work to which Robert has committed, the work of re-imaging his sense of self, of walking across the abyss which we are, on the rope we must invent by our imaginal courage.

If we carry our Hell with us, and reconstitute it by our repetition compulsion, then we must also carry the Lord of the Underworld as well. When St. Paul says he knows the good but does not do the good, why not? The Christian might say we are prone to sin, to fall into a bad choice through some perversity of will. Plato and Platonists through the years, the Deists of the eighteenth century, and many liberal reformers in the nineteenth and twentieth centuries, claim we do not do the good out of ignorance. If we were better educated, more conscious, they say, we would choose the good. Others, from Nietzsche and Dostoyevsky to depth psychologists, testify to a shadow energy which is outside ego control and may even seduce the ego into collusion. Thus, "good" values may serve dark ends.

There was a large sign at Dachau which read, "There is a road to freedom, its milestones are: Obedience, Industry, Honesty, Order, Cleanliness, Sobriety, Sincerity, and a Spirit of Sacrifice and Patriotism." Our capacity to take virtues and turn them upside down to serve such a place is staggering. But what devil do we carry who works to produce such evil in the name of good?

In a functional way, the devil we must confront is within; we carry it everywhere, and it insinuates its power into our every act. Such a devil is the embodiment of the autonomy of our own history. Jung observed that we are "as much possessed by [our] pathological states as any witch or witch-hunter in the darkest Middle Ages. It is merely a difference of name. In those days they spoke of the devil, today we call it a neurosis."[89] What happened to us, how we interpreted our experience and internalized our understanding of it, is now rooted within us and causes us to reconstitute an ever-renewing Hell.

"Myself am Hell." As long as our devil remains unnamed, left to toil unhampered in the caverns of the unconscious, we will do its work. Such a force is working within Robert to tie him forever to his mother, to the child on the gurney, and to doom his relationships. He is lost unless he can name his devil, confront it in every hour in the fight of his entire life for a more abundant imago of selfhood. It is in this sense that St. Paul writes, in Acts 26:18, that the task is to open one's eyes and throw off the work of darkness, move from the satanic power to the divine freedom. And it is in this sense that Satish Kumar observed:

> The mind is a very dubious instrument. If it is kept in check, it is a useful tool. But if it is not kept in check, it creates problems. It is an efficient machine that can manufacture millions and millions of problems without any raw materials! So we create problems and then make ourselves victims of the problems we have created. That is the battle that is co-created by the mind. . . . I am my own hell, the maker of my own problems.[90]

Only the person who has reached a substantial level of maturity can acknowledge this paradox, that he or she now is the enemy. One needs to reach at least the middle years before one can take on the immensity of this project. One needs to have made projections onto the outer world—career, relationships, social roles—and suffered their insufficiency; one needs to have made enough mistakes to begin to see a pattern; one needs to have attained a strong enough ego to dare look within for the source of one's choices. Only then does one have the experience, and the courage, to sort through, to differentiate, the unconscious causal factors and then

---

[89] "The Meaning of Psychology for Modern Man," *Civilization in Transition,* CW 10, par. 309.
[90] "Longing for Loneliness," p. 10.

to make a break for a new life.

While it takes until midlife until one has suffered or matured enough to begin the task of consciousness, the middle passage has otherwise little to do with one's chronological age. The encounter with one's own autonomous history begins when one is forced to begin it.

Julia was long widowed and had worked very painfully to move back out into life after losing her companion. Far greater than her grief, which was considerable, was the task of claiming her own authority and finding a personal life wisdom. Early in life Julia had learned to defer her own truth to her omnipotent and omniscient father. She had searched for and married a man who carried on the mantle of external authority. With both father and husband gone, Julia felt abandoned, not only by these "authorities" but by the universe itself which now seemed hostile and alien. Concurrently, she had to face her own aging and declining health, the specter of mortality.

Her therapy involved a progressive movement toward personal empowerment and a greater philosophical embrace of the universe. By "philosophical" I do not mean a cognitive structure, or even a religious belief, each of which has its value, but rather an emotional enlargement. Julia's life had been dominated by the father complex. Benign though it seemed, it had kept her from her own psychological adulthood. Growing up required the enlargement of her sense of self beyond the little girl who needed Daddy to protect and guide her. She was the abyss and the rope across. Shortly before terminating her analysis, Julia had the following dream. When she brought it in she said that it sounded as if she had made it up, but she had recorded it just as she had experienced it.

> I am out walking. As I turn to the left I find a curious chalk or white stone landscape. There are white stone hills, white stone roads, and even houses cut out of the chalklike stone, like the Pueblo houses. It is not a luxury neighborhood, nor is it a slum. There seems no life, no greenery, no color.
>
> As I walk on I find the road is Main Street. I come to an exhibit: a fair or market of all kinds of things. . . . Everyone is friendly and talks to me. There is a chair with a big dog that is obviously mourning its master and is grateful that we pay it attention.
>
> It seems to me that the chalk-white development and the market are the juxtaposition of all that is human. There is much sentiment attached to the

market, but all of it is passing. The white stone is probably lasting forever, but it is not full of affection like the dog and the bits of human memorabilia.

Julia's feeling-toned reaction to the dream was of great calm, great acceptance. She felt this was a "philosophical" dream, less in what was said, but what was shown, experienced in a new way, and absorbed. She was quick to grasp the polarities of the dream, the eternal white stone city and the passionate marketplace of life, what Yeats called "the fury and mire of human veins."[91] In sheltering from her journey under the powerful and protective wings of father and husband, she had not fully taken on her own life, not chanced the abyss.

Julia's dream embraces the opposites. To be in life is to suffer its losses, to dwell in the swamplands, yet to gain the fullest measure of wisdom is to see what it transcends as well. Julia seemed different after that dream; it proved more than a concept to her. The wisdom of that activity of soul in her which had brought the tension of opposites into a dream enabled her to break the old paradigm and live an enlarged life. She was able to make larger choices coming from a larger imaginal self. She still suffered grief, loss, angst, but she also knew that her twin task was to be in life, and, like the grieving, faithful dog, also to suffer the loss of her master, and then know the white stone city which exists beyond loss.

Unbeknown to Julia, Rilke had written a poem about loss, evanescence and the perception of the "white city":

> All is far
> And long gone by.
> I believe the star
> That shines up there
> Has been dead for a thousand years. . . .
> I would like to walk
> Out of my heart, under the great sky.
> I would like to pray.
> And surely, of all the stars,
> One still must be.
> I believe I know
> Which one endures;

---

[91] "Byzantium," in *Selected Poems and Two Plays,* p. 132.

> Which one, at the end of its beam in the sky,
> Stands like a white city.[92]

Amid the flux and flow of life's energy, passing, always passing, a vision of the white city is vouchsafed only to those who have "gone through" the swampland of loss.

There is an incredible sweetness that comes to those who have "gone through," though one could not begin to imagine such a thing while enduring the torments of Hell. I immediately think of Oedipus at Colonus, Yeats toward the end of his life, and my own dream that anticipated healing.[93] Allegedly in his ninetieth year, Sophocles returned to the theme of Oedipus, the tragic story of the wounded history which, operating unconsciously, wounds subsequent generations. When all comes to catastrophe, Oedipus is cast into exile and wanders alone and penitent for many years. Through his suffering he achieves a humbled relationship with the gods and, when he comes to die at Colonus, he is granted an apotheosis and is blessed by them. And thus the blind but redeemed Oedipus, one who has "gone through," is able to say, "Suffering and time, vast time, have been instructors in contentment."[94] And Yeats, aging and in poor health, surveys the turbulent course of his life and in 1929 concludes,

> We must laugh and we must sing,
> We are blest by everything,
> Everything we look upon is blest.[95]

No young person could write such lines. We must wait decades and put our lives on the line, be tested and come through. The above lines come at the end of a long text which acknowledges the defeats, disappointments and losses of Yeats's life. No shallow optimism there, only the deepened wisdom of a person who spent much of this life in the swamplands, and from that miasmic material forged his life and his art.

At a critical moment in my analytical training, when it seemed that for

---

[92] "Lament," in Flores, ed., *An Anthology of German Poetry,* p. 386.

[93] Above, p. 46.

[94] Sophocles, *Oedipus at Colonus,* in *The Complete Greek Tragedies,* p. 79.

[95] "A Dialogue of Self and Soul," in *Selected Poems and Two Plays,* p. 126.

many reasons, not the least financial, I would be unable to continue, I had a dream that moved me deeply. The critical motif occurred as my son Tim and I walked through the lovely, hundred-foot-tall pine forests which were at that time covered with snow. Tim said to me, "When you have suffered enough, and stood as tall as these trees, then the snow will be a gift to you as a mantle of grace."

The way in which the trees were rendered even more beautiful by their mantilla of snow certainly did convey a sense of a graceful gift. My feeling response was that if I found a way to carry on, to go through, that I might be granted that mantle of grace. My son, himself a graceful gift to me, was also the inner symbol of my best, future possibilities. The dream itself was a gift and played no small part in my getting through a difficult time.

It is no accident that I have turned to dreams, and to the wisdom of great writers, in looking at the swamplands. Those of us who follow our dreams know there is a rich, resonant autonomous activity going on in the psyche. Just as we are pulled down into the swamplands of doubt and despair and the other dismal dozen, so too are we graced with healing images that seek to compensate, redirect and develop the conscious personality. Just as we are obliged to suffer, so we can move through to deeper meaning. Just as Jung said neurosis is suffering which has not yet found its meaning, so we are spared neither the suffering nor the task of working through to its meaning. Just as Rilke in his life and art, and Julia in her dream, glimpsed the timeless white city, so we are able to find the support of the psyche in our struggle through the abysmal swamps.

Another remarkable dream will illustrate. It seemed more didactic than many, but the dreamer insisted she had not embellished it in any way. As an introductory note to the dream she wrote that "the experience is a play that happens in multiple locations *simultaneously*. You wander around and *experience* it in different locations, always getting only a slice or sliver of the whole. *You* have to put it together, *make sense of it.*"

The dream ran to several pages. Here are the salient features:

> I arrive at the last minute and grab a seat as far forward as I can. This seems more a play reading than a display of action. You can only hear, not see what happens except for a peephole in the wall. I move to a better

view. I receive a lot of notes and documents about the play and I scan each one, angry that they put all this at the front rather than the end of the play. I find several maps, helpful for locating what actions are taking place. This might make more sense of the whole.

Two men whisper some dialogue from the play. There is the feeling of some conspiracy afoot. I'm annoyed because I can't hear the whole play. I try to find my stuff and move my seat again. I am annoyed at the difficulty in understanding the play. Then I begin to remember the little I had heard about it, that it was to be experienced on multiple fronts. You gather clues as you go, and try to put it together from many glimpses.

Then we are told to fiddle with our fingers, which I find silly and futile. Why bother? Then I get an insight—to make space for something else, something new, that's why you fiddle with your fingers. Okay, now I get it, wander around and see the play, listen everywhere, and see what you can put together.

[The dream shifts to a different scene where a camel is being lead along by "camel eggs."]

The camel eggs got dropped and broken! Just then an adult man came up from the direction in which we were heading. What a tragedy. Then I realized, *no, not a tragedy!* (Only an apparent tragedy.) The eggs were to lead us this far, to this moment. *Now they aren't needed anymore. We're ready for the next leading, the next insight.* [Italics are the dreamer's.]

Evelyn, the dreamer, is a fifty-eight-year-old woman who has always been aware of the need to find her own path. Like us all, she would have preferred certainties but found only fragments, disappointments, a painful divorce, the need to raise her children and find a job, but most of all the need to find her own truth. Like us all, she would have preferred to be given the big picture clearly, coherently and quickly. Like us all, she has had to painfully piece things together over decades. Like Julia's dream of the white city, this dream suggests that we are present to the unfolding drama, but we get only bits and pieces of it. It is never really clear, our vision never unobstructed, our understanding never complete.

But the dream-ego begins to figure out that that is the nature of the play: experience it on multiple fronts, gather insights along the way, make space for something new—keep fiddling with it. The absurdity of this was beyond Evelyn's understanding, yet she felt it represented some activity of her own which might seem meaningless, but which in time would lead to some new breakthrough. The act of meditating occurred to her as an analogy. Nothing happens, one feels stagnant, and then there is movement.

With the camel Evelyn associated "the ship of the desert," the capacity to survive the long trek, often across arid regions. The eggs represented her potential, what could be hatched. But most of these eggs are broken, pointing to past activities that had brought her this far, but which no longer served her. Among those now broken eggs she cited her marriage, her mothering role, an earlier career, her push-pull dependency on her parents, and numerous activities in the community. She said the eggs were "all the leads that got me this far—that's all they were meant to do, not to be continued forever."

This is a very wise dream and a wise conclusion. We never achieve final certainty, never see the whole picture, never arrive at the sun-lit meadow. We see through the glass darkly, see bits and pieces only. Yeats said it well:

> I made my song a coat
> Covered with embroideries
> Out of old mythologies.[96]

So we patch such experiences together and wear them into the world. Evelyn's search for certainty, her desire for the big picture, her need for outer direction and authority are all frustrated. But she is given a vision of why one is obliged to go through the swamplands. She understands there are only fragments, many broken eggs, but all were valuable, all have meaning. Like the visitant to the white city, she has been invited to the Great Play in which we are but tiny actors.

Hindus say the world is God's play. The vision of transcendence may not be clear, but the task of catching glimpses, hatching new eggs along the way, suffering the arid places of the soul, leads in the end to the realization that the meaning is not in the arrival but in the journey itself. That is the wisdom of a person who "goes through." No one who is young, who demands resolution of the raggedy edges of life, or who flees the task implicit in all suffering, can "go through" and receive this wisdom. As with Oedipus and Yeats, it is a reward the youthful ego would scorn

---

[96] "A Coat," ibid., p. 50.

and can never comprehend, but it is the gift that brings depth, maturity and a rich aura to later life.

The task confronting Robert, Julia, Evelyn, us all, is the same task that Nietzsche set out for us in the last century. We are "a going-under" and we are a "bridge." What has to go under is the ego's desire for control, for dominance, for security. As natural as that desire might be, it also stands in the way of transformation. The bridging required is from the child's desire to cling to any security, to avoid stepping out into the unknown world. Our boat is so small, the ocean so great. And yet the most formidable obstacle remains the constriction of personal history, the limited Weltanschauung of the complexes.

One of the reasons we revere discoverers, explorers and pioneers in the physical world, and those who push back the limits of mind or aesthetic expression, is because they carry for us the archetype of the hero, that complex of energy in all of us that naturally seeks to pose itself against the regressive powers of fear and lethargy in the service of individuation. When an outer hero exemplifies such action, we find a resonant energy within ourselves to similarly push back the limitations of the known. This is what Nietzsche meant by crossing the abyss on the tightrope of ourselves. The energy is there, the task is to risk walking further out into space. In that space is more freedom, a greater amplitude of soul; it is where we are meant to be.

Afterword
The Blur and Blot of Life

The dread and resistance which every natural human being experiences when it comes to delving too deeply into himself is, at bottom, the fear of the journey to Hades.—C.G. Jung.

What is to be gained from these unwelcome descents to Hades? If there are lessons here, what are they? Running throughout this book are three ideas or principles which, if we accept them and the agenda they imply, can lead us toward an enlarged psychic life.

The first principle is that due to the natural ebb and flow of psychic energy we will inevitably and frequently be pulled down, against our will, into dark places. Just as a drowsy child fights going to sleep until at last overwhelmed, so we identify with the frangible ego and its under-standable albeit futile quest for permanent security. As that ego is pulled down into the depths, we experience it as a kind of defeat and fault our-selves for our symptoms. We feel shamed by our panic attacks, degraded by our depression and furtive about our fears—as if everyone else were not beset by those same psychic invasions.

Thus it is essential for us to accept that *our psychic life will frequently act outside the control of the ego, that we will be pulled down into the swamplands, and that we will suffer there.* No amount of denial, no amount of anesthetizing, no "good work and right thinking" will spare us. The modern fantasy of "happiness" is pernicious because it is not only impossible to attain and hold but may in fact render us even more neurotic and attached to our wounds.

The second principle is that *in each of these swampland states there is an implicit challenge to discover its meaning and the change of behavior or attitude it may oblige.* Confronting each swampland as an implicit question—what is the meaning of my depression, to what is the anxiety linked in my history, what am I possessed by—allows us to be active in-stead of passive in our suffering. During this struggle we move from the fantasy of permanent happiness, or shame at not achieving it, to what is

141

perhaps the greatest gift—the knowledge that we can live without happiness, but not without meaning.

In articulating the task in each swampland, we "go through" suffering toward an enlarged consciousness. As mentioned earlier, Jung understood neurosis as suffering which has not found its meaning.[97] We cannot be spared suffering, only the neurotic round in which we swamp and stall without being enriched.

The third principle animating this book is that *as our characteristic response patterns to swampland stress is reflexive in character, tied to past experience, we are obliged to re-imagine ourselves in order to live in the present.*

There is a broad spectrum of responses possible to the conscious adult living in the present, but the activated complexes shrink our vision to the narrow range determined by our regressive reflexes. We cannot be spared the activity of complexes, for we have a life history affectively charged with memory, a vision of the world, and a learned set of attitudes and behaviors. Some of our complex reactions are even helpful to us, save our lives, allow us to bond with others or affirm values. Others are wholly negative in their effects. The most primal complexes are, naturally, derivative of earliest experience and would therefore constrict us to the vision and reactions of a child.

Recall, then, the strange image presented by Nietzsche, that we are the abyss and also the rope across it. The abyss is our terrible freedom, the largeness of our journey which so intimidates, while the rope has to do with how we are able to re-image ourselves beyond what was possible in the past. If we are limited to the capacities of our family of origin, our culture or our personal history, then we are truly passive sufferers of fate. If we can redefine ourselves, step into the abyss, walk across this imaginal extension of psyche, then we may more fully claim our lives.

We all cling to two impossible fantasies, that of immortality and that of the Magical Other. Notice that death is not one of the swampland states discussed in this book, though surely some awareness of death, perhaps preoccupation with it, haunts each day. Since the ego seeks se-

---

[97] Above, p. 9.

curity, stability and control, death is the greatest threat, the darkest antagonist. Perhaps death will be a great release from the ego's petty preoccupations, a liberation, a transcendence. If the Hindus are right one will recycle in some other incarnation toward a final liberation of soul. If the Buddhists are right, death is a bad dream, a *trompe d'oeil,* a delusion of the ego. If one can transcend the ego's imperialism, then one may transcend the false life-death dichotomy from which we suffer. If the Christians are right, there is an afterlife. If the Jews are right we survive through our descendants. Whatever one's belief, the encounter with personal mortality provides a point of reference that lends depth to life—a soul perspective on who we are and what we do.

All we can say for sure is that a mystery courses through us, seeking its own fullest incarnation, and that whenever we serve the mystery within we experience a linkage to the mystery outside. When we stand in conscious relationship to this mystery, we are more deeply alive. Though the ego may be flooded from time to time with existential angst, we know that the ego is only a tiny part of the soul. When the imperial ego can bow to a willing partnership with the rest of the psyche, then the individual is more at ease with the larger mystery.

How insufferable the ego would be if it could claim immortality, but as Shakespeare noted, "Golden lads and girls all must, / As chimney-sweepers, come to dust."[98] Death, then, is not a swampland, though our angst is. Death is that which makes humble wisdom possible.

The other fantasy, that of the Magical Other, the hope that someone out there will rescue us, spare us our journey, make our lives work, is nearly as ubiquitous. The popularity of the book and film *The Bridges of Madison County* is an expression of this pernicious hope, that some day a stranger will appear in our back yard, make wonderful love to us and thereby provide the connection with soul for which we long.

The prolonged indulgence in such a fantasy assures that we will remain locked in infantile thinking. It is a legacy of the child's dependence on the parent, which quite naturally becomes the implicit model for all future relationships. So we transfer the paradigm of powerful parent onto

---

[98] *Cymbeline,* act 4, scene 2.

the Other. More than anything else, this fantasy, this transference of an early agenda, sabotages relationship. It is not just that our complexes contaminate what begins freshly and with such promise, but that we grow angry, frustrated and bitter toward the other for not fulfilling this great hidden agenda, our unreachable expectations.

Ultimately, the Magical Other, were we to find such a person, would be our greatest threat for he or she would keep us from our fuller selves. A wise analysand said to me just yesterday that she was learning to give up her "addiction to hope." While she still looks forward to a meaningful relationship, she has gained the strength to let go of the addictive fantasy of the Magical Other. Her letting go is what T.S. Eliot meant by, "Wait without hope / for hope would be hope for the wrong thing."[99]

Both fantasies, of immortality and magical rescue, impede our engagement with this life, the here-and-now. If we have been blessed by the gods to reach midlife and beyond, we will have gone through considerable suffering to be sure, but we will also have been granted the capacity for revisioning ourselves. This revisioning will require visits not only to Parnassus, or Athens, or Jerusalem or Zürich, but to the swamplands as well, from which we will learn the most. If we have lived to midlife and beyond, we have a chance to experience wisdom. It will not be the sort of wisdom the ego would prefer, mastery over all, but it will be richer than any ego could envision. "Strait is the gate, and narrow is the way, which leadeth unto life." (Matt. 7:14)

Each of us has been offered a journey. Each of us is responsible for the fullest possible expression of this individuation imperative. While we need to do this work on a conscious, daily basis in any case, we may also choose to facilitate it with a therapist companion. The therapist, too, comes wounded into the relationship, but we have every right to expect that he or she will have worked on their wounds and be able to accompany us wisely. For both, slogging through the swamp can be a humbling and precious experience. Jung wrote,

> The principle aim of psychotherapy is not to transport the patient to an impossible state of happiness, but to help him acquire steadfastness and

---

[99] *The Four Quartets*, p. 126.

philosophic patience in the face of suffering. Life demands for its completion and fulfilment a balance between joy and sorrow. But because suffering is positively disagreeable, people naturally prefer not to ponder how much fear and sorrow fall to the lot of man. So they speak soothingly about progress and the greatest possible happiness, forgetting that happiness is itself poisoned if the measure of suffering has not been fulfilled. Behind a neurosis there is so often concealed all the natural and necessary suffering the patient has been unwilling to bear.[100]

In our separate suffering we are together in a joint journey. But we do have the journey. Jung reminds us:

The achievement of personality . . . . is an act of high courage flung in the face of life, the absolute affirmation of all that constitutes the individual, the most successful adaptation to the universal conditions of existence coupled with the greatest possible freedom for self-determination.[101]

Moreover, he says, "Each individual is a new experiment of life in her ever-changing moods, and an attempt at a new solution or new adaptation."[102] Our work in the swamplands is what creates the new adaptation that furthers the life force.

Jung also notes that every neurosis is "an offended god,"[103] by which he means that some archetypal principle is violated. In taking on the task implicit in every swampland, we make possible the reclamation of the divine. Why do I say "divine"? Because the activity of the psyche is inherently religious. It seeks connection, meaning, transcendence. It is the most profound of paradoxes that we may discover these divine principles less on mountain tops, less in cathedrals, than in swamplands.

For all its transcendent mystery, life is also a blur and a blot. We never see it really clearly. We never get it all right; we never get it fixed; we never get it finished.

Jennifer was visiting her dying mother in Minneapolis. She got on the plane dreading the encounter, for her mother had always sought to de-

---

[100] "Psychotherapy and a Philosophy of Life," *The Practice of Psychotherapy*, CW 16, par. 185.
[101] "The Development of Personality," *The Development of Personality*, CW 17, par. 289.
[102] "Analytical Psychology and Education," ibid., par. 173.
[103] *Two Essays on Analytical Psychology*, CW 7, par. 392.

vour her—yet now she was dying. "Contained openness . . . contained openness," became Jennifer's mantra. She chanted this on the plane, in the airport, in the elevator at the hospital. She sought to be open to her mother, emotionally available to her in her hour of need, and yet to contain herself psychologically so that she not be savaged yet again.

Face to face with her mother, Jennifer could do little more than barely contain her suspicion and anger, and so left her for the last time with a deep sense of failure. Months later, she was flooded with dreams and flashbacks of that final encounter. She berated herself for her defensiveness, her casualness, her emotional distancing, her inability to cry with her mother and tell her she loved her. She knew she had lived only half of her mantra, more contained than open.

So, we never get it all right. The blur and blot of it, too fast, too complex, too obscure. Only now and then is there clarity, purpose, victory. For surely we are not gods, though the godly courses within us just as the demonic does. It is a wonder we survive at all, that we have moments of peace, of kindness toward others, even occasionally a bit of charity toward ourselves.

Shall we fault Jennifer as much as she condemns herself? We will tell her that that last meeting took place in the context of a hurtful history. She will reply that she was plunged into the same old swampland and responded in the same old way, that she had not been up to the transcendent requirement and opportunity of the moment. And then we will ask her to do what we ourselves find hardest, to forgive herself for being human.

In the final analysis we do not solve our problems, for life is not a problem to be solved but an experiment to be lived. It is enough to have suffered through into deeper and deeper meaning. Such meaning enriches and is its own reward. We cannot avoid the swamplands of the soul, but we may come to value them for what they can bring us.

> We must be still and still moving
> Into another intensity
> For a further union, a deeper communion
> Through the dark cold and the empty desolation.[104]

---

[104] Eliot, *The Four Quartets*, p. 129.

Bibliography

Arnold, Matthew. *Poetry and Criticism of Matthew Arnold.* Ed. A. Dwight Culler. New York: Houghton-Mifflin, 1961.

Auden, W.H. *Collected Poems.* New York: Random House, 1976.

Bateson, Gregory. *Steps to an Ecology of Mind.* New York: Ballantine, 1972.

Bauer, Jan. *Alcoholism and Women: The Background and the Psychology.* Toronto: Inner City Books, 1982.

Bonhoeffer, Dietrich. *Letters and Papers from Prison.* New York: MacMillan, 1972.

Camus, Albert. *The Fall.* Trans. Justin O'Brien. New York: Vintage Books, 1956.

_____. *The Myth of Sisyphus.* Trans. Justin O'Brien. New York: Alfred A. Knopf, 1955.

Carotenuto, Aldo. *The Difficult Art: A Critical Discourse on Psychotherapy.* Trans. Joan Tambuseno. Wilmette, IL: Chiron Publications, 1992.

_____. *Eros and Pathos: Shades of Love and Suffering.* Toronto: Inner City Books, 1989.

The Complete Greek Tragedies. Trans. Robert Fitzgerald. Chicago: University of Chicao Press, 1957.

Cooper, M. Truman. "Fearing Paris." In *River City,* vol. 9, no. 1 (Spring 1989).

Corneau, Guy. *Absent Fathers, Lost Sons: The Search for Masculine Identity.* Boston: Shambhala Publications, 1991.

Edinger, Edward F. *The Creation of Consciousness: Jung's Myth for Modern Man.* Toronto: Inner City Books, 1984.

Eliot, T.S. *The Four Quartets.* In *T.S. Eliot: The Complete Poems and Plays, 1909-1950.* New York: Harcourt, Brace, and World, 1962.

Flores, Angel, trans. and ed. *An Anthology of French Poetry from de Nerval to Valéry.* New York: Doubleday Anchor, 1962.

_____. *An Anthology of German Poetry from Hölderlin to Rilke.* New York: Doubleday Anchor, 1960.

Frankl, Victor. *Man's Search for Meaning.* New York: Simon and Schuster, 1959.

Frost, Robert. *Modern Poems.* Ed. Richard Ellmann and Robert O'Clair. New York: W.W. Norton, 1973.

_____. *Robert Frost's Poems*. Ed. Louis Untermeyer. New York: Washington Square Press, 1962.

Heidegger, Martin. *Existence and Being*. Trans. Werner Brock. Chicago: Henry Regnery, 1949.

Hesse, Hermann. *The Glass Bead Game*. New York: Holt, Rinehart and Winston, 1969.

Hillman, James. *Suicide and the Soul*. Zürich: Spring Publications, 1976.

Hollis, James. *The Middle Passage: From Misery to Meaning in Midlife*. Toronto: Inner City Books, 1993.

_____. *Tracking the Gods: The Place of Myth in Modern Life*. Toronto: Inner City Books, 1995.

_____. *Under Saturn's Shadow: The Wounding and Healing of Men*. Toronto: Inner City Books, 1994.

Jung, C.G. *The Collected Works* (Bollingen Series XX). 20 vols. Trans. R.F.C. Hull. Ed. H. Read, M. Fordham, G. Adler, Wm. McGuire. Princeton: Princeton University Press, 1953-1979.

_____. *Memories, Dreams, Reflections*. Ed. Aniela Jaffé. New York: Pantheon Books, 1961.

Kafka, Franz. *The Diaries of Franz Kafka, 1914-23*. Trans. Martin Greenberg. Ed. Max Brod. London: Secker and Warburg, 1949.

Kazantzakis, Nikos. *The Saviors of God*. Trans. Kimon Friar. New York: Simon and Schuster, 1960.

Kierkegaard, Sören. *Fear and Trembling*. New York: Doubleday, 1954.

Kliewer, Warren. *Liturgies, Games, Farewells*. Francestown, NH: The Golden Quill Press, 1974.

Kumar, Satish. "Longing for Wholeness." In *Parabola*, vol. 20, no. 2 (1995).

Machado, Antonio. *Times Alone*. Trans. Robert Bly. Middletown, CT: Wesleyan University Press, 1983.

MacLeish, Archibald. *J.B.* Boston: Houghton-Mifflin, 1958.

Modern American and British Poetry. Ed. Louis Untermeyer. New York: Harcourt, Brace, 1955.

Mood, John. *Rilke On Love and Other Difficulties*. New York: W.W. Norton, 1975.

Moustakis, Clark E. *Loneliness*. New York: Prentice-Hall, 1961.

Nietzsche, Friedrich. *The Portable Nietzsche*. Trans. Walter Kaufmann. New York: Viking Press, 1968.

Norton Anthology of Poetry. Ed. A. Alison. New York: W.W. Norton, 1970.

The Oxford Dictionary of Quotations. Ed. Bernard Darwin. Oxford: Oxford University Press, 1980.

Pascal. *Pensées.* New York: E.P. Dutton and Co., 1958.

Reynolds, David S. *Walt Whitman's America.* New York: Alfred A. Knopf, 1995.

Rilke, Rainer Maria. *Duino Elegies.* Trans. J.B. Leishman and Stephen Spender. New York: Norton, 1967.

_____. *Letters to a Young Poet.* Trans. M.D. Herter Norton. New York: Norton and Norton, 1954.

Sharp, Daryl. *The Survival Papers: Anatomy of a Midlife Crisis.* Toronto: Inner City Books, 1988.

_____. *Who Am I, Really? Personality, Soul and Individuation.* Toronto: Inner City Books, 1995.

Shelley, Percy Bysshe. *The Poems of Shelley.* Oxford: Oxford University Press, 1960.

Tillich, Paul. *The Dynamics of Faith.* New York: Harper, 1957.

_____. *The Shaking of the Foundations.* New York: Charles Scribner's Sons, 1948.

Tillyard, E.M.W. *The Elizabethan World Picture.* New York: Vintage Books, 1954.

Wolfe, Thomas. *The Hills Beyond.* New York: Harper and Brothers, 1941.

Woodman, Marion. *Addiction to Perfection: The Still Unravished Bride.* Toronto: Inner City Books, 1982.

Yeats, W.B. *Selected Poems and Two Plays of William Butler Yeats.* Ed. M. L. Rosenthal. New York: MacMillan, 1962.

Zoja, Luigi. *Growth and Guilt: Psychology and the Limits of Development.* New York: Routledge, 1995.

Zorn, Fritz. *Mars.* New York: Alfred A. Knopf, 1982.

Index

151

Studies in Jungian Psychology
by Jungian Analysts

Quality Paperbacks

Prices and payment in $US (except in Canada, $Cdn)

1. The Secret Raven: Conflict and Transformation
Daryl Sharp (Toronto). ISBN 0-919123-00-7. 128 pp. $16

2. The Psychological Meaning of Redemption Motifs in Fairy Tales
Marie-Louise von Franz (Zürich). ISBN 0-919123-01-5. 128 pp. $16

3. On Divination and Synchronicity: The Psychology of Meaningful Chance
Marie-Louise von Franz (Zürich). ISBN 0-919123-02-3. 128 pp. $16

4. The Owl Was a Baker's Daughter: Obesity, Anorexia and the Repressed Feminine Marion Woodman (Toronto). ISBN 0-919123-03-1. 144 pp. $16

5. Alchemy: An Introduction to the Symbolism and the Psychology
Marie-Louise von Franz (Zürich). ISBN 0-919123-04-X. 288 pp. $20

6. Descent to the Goddess: A Way of Initiation for Women
Sylvia Brinton Perera (New York). ISBN 0-919123-05-8. 112 pp. $16

7. The Psyche as Sacrament: A Comparative Study of C.G. Jung and Paul Tillich John P. Dourley (Ottawa). ISBN 0-919123-06-6. 128 pp. $16

8. Border Crossings: Carlos Castaneda's Path of Knowledge
Donald Lee Williams (Boulder). ISBN 0-919123-07-4. 160 pp. $16

9. Narcissism and Character Transformation: The Psychology of Narcissistic Character Disorders
Nathan Schwartz-Salant (New York). ISBN 0-919123-08-2. 192 pp. $18

10. Rape and Ritual: A Psychological Study
Bradley A. Te Paske (Santa Barbara). ISBN 0-919123-09-0. 160 pp. $16

11. Alcoholism and Women: The Background and the Psychology
Jan Bauer (Montreal). ISBN 0-919123-10-4. 144 pp. $16

12. Addiction to Perfection: The Still Unravished Bride
Marion Woodman (Toronto). ISBN 0-919123-11-2. 208 pp. $18pb/$25hc

13. Jungian Dream Interpretation: A Handbook of Theory and Practice
James A. Hall, M.D. (Dallas). ISBN 0-919123-12-0. 128 pp. $16

14. The Creation of Consciousness: Jung's Myth for Modern Man
Edward F. Edinger (Los Angeles). ISBN 0-919123-13-9. 128 pp. $16

15. The Analytic Encounter: Transference and Human Relationship
Mario Jacoby (Zürich). ISBN 0-919123-14-7. 128 pp. $16

16. Change of Life: Dreams and the Menopause
Ann Mankowitz (Ireland). ISBN 0-919123-15-5. 128 pp. $16

17. The Illness That We Are: A Jungian Critique of Christianity
John P. Dourley (Ottawa). ISBN 0-919123-16-3. 128 pp. $16

18. Hags and Heroes: A Feminist Approach to Jungian Psychotherapy with Couples Polly Young-Eisendrath (Philadelphia). ISBN 0-919123-17-1. 192 pp. $18

19. Cultural Attitudes in Psychological Perspective
Joseph L. Henderson, M.D. (San Francisco). ISBN 0-919123-18-X. 128 pp. $16

20. The Vertical Labyrinth: Individuation in Jungian Psychology
Aldo Carotenuto (Rome). ISBN 0-919123-19-8. 144 pp. $16

44. The Dream Story
Donald Broadribb (Baker's Hill, Australia). ISBN 0-919123-45-7.   256 pp. $20

45. The Rainbow Serpent: Bridge to Consciousness
Robert L. Gardner (Toronto). ISBN 0-919123-46-5.   128 pp. $16

46. Circle of Care: Clinical Issues in Jungian Therapy
Warren Steinberg (New York). ISBN 0-919123-47-3.   160 pp. $16

47. Jung Lexicon: A Primer of Terms & Concepts
Daryl Sharp (Toronto). ISBN 0-919123-48-1.   160 pp. $16

48. Body and Soul: The Other Side of Illness
Albert Kreinheder (Los Angeles). ISBN 0-919123-49-X.   112 pp. $16

49. Animus Aeternus: Exploring the Inner Masculine
Deldon Anne McNeely (Lynchburg, VA). ISBN 0-919123-50-3.   192 pp. $18

50. Castration and Male Rage: The Phallic Wound
Eugene Monick (Scranton, PA). ISBN 0-919123-51-1.   144 pp. $16

51. Saturday's Child: Encounters with the Dark Gods
Janet O. Dallett (Seal Harbor, WA). ISBN 0-919123-52-X.   128 pp. $16

52. The Secret Lore of Gardening: Patterns of Male Intimacy
Graham Jackson (Toronto). ISBN 0-919123-53-8.   160 pp. $16

53. The Refiner's Fire: Memoirs of a German Girlhood
Sigrid R. McPherson (Los Angeles). ISBN 0-919123-54-6.   208 pp. $18

54. Transformation of the God-Image: Jung's *Answer to Job*
Edward F. Edinger (Los Angeles). ISBN 0-919123-55-4.   144 pp. $16

55. Getting to Know You: The Inside Out of Relationship
Daryl Sharp (Toronto). ISBN 0-919123-56-2.   128 pp. $16

56. A Strategy for a Loss of Faith: Jung's Proposal
John P. Dourley (Ottawa). ISBN 0-919123-57-0.   144 pp. $16

57. Close Relationships: Family, Friendship, Marriage
Eleanor Bertine (New York). ISBN 0-919123-58-9.   160 pp. $16

58. Conscious Femininity: Interviews with Marion Woodman
Introduction by Marion Woodman (Toronto). ISBN 0-919123-59-7.   160 pp. $16

59. The Middle Passage: From Misery to Meaning in Midlife
James Hollis (Houston). ISBN 0-919123-60-0.   128 pp. $16

60. The Living Room Mysteries: Patterns of Male Intimacy, Book 2
Graham Jackson (Toronto). ISBN 0-919123-61-9.   144 pp. $16

61. Chicken Little: The Inside Story *(A Jungian Romance)*
Daryl Sharp (Toronto). ISBN 0-919123-62-7.   128 pp. $16

62. Coming To Age: The Croning Years and Late-Life Transformation
Jane R. Prétat (Providence, RI). ISBN 0-919123-63-5.   144 pp. $16

63. Under Saturn's Shadow: The Wounding and Healing of Men
James Hollis (Houston). ISBN 0-919123-64-3.   144 pp. $16

Discounts: any 3-5 books, 10%; 6-9 books, 20%; 10 or more, 25%
Add Postage/Handling: 1-2 books, $3; 3-4 books, $5; 5-9 books, $10; 10 or more, free

Write or phone for free Catalogue of **over 80 titles** and **Jung at Heart** newsletter

INNER CITY BOOKS

Box 1271, Station Q, Toronto, ON M4T 2P4, Canada   **(416) 927-0355**